REFINING THROUGH FAILURE
THE GUIDE

REFINING THROUGH FAILURE
THE GUIDE

C. LLOYD BROWN

Copyright © C. Lloyd Brown, 2023

All rights reserved. No part of this book may be reproduced in any form on by an electronic or mechanical means, including information storage and retrieval systems, without permission in writing from the publisher, except by a reviewer who may quote brief passages in a review.

This is a work of creative nonfiction. Some parts have been fictionalized in varying degrees, for various purposes.

ISBN 979-8-218-28526-5 (paperback)
ISBN 979-8-218-28527-2 (ebook)

First Edition: September 2023

This paperback edition first published in 2023

This book is dedicated to all the people in my life who have been with me through my failures, and still choose to be with me. Especially my wife, Lora.

Contents

Foreword 9
Introduction 11

1. **What is Your Story?** 13
   Activity: Writing Your Own Story 16
   Activity: Evaluating Your Decisions 25
   Activity: Choosing a Trusted Advisor 28
2. **Why We Do What We Do** 31
   Activity: "I Am" 33
   Activity: Starting with Why 37
   Activity: Personal Belief Script 45
   Activity: Your Personal Belief Matrix 48
3. **How Relationships Impact Your Life** 51
   Activity: Define and Classify Key Relationships 56
4. **Defining Our Rules and Boundaries** 59
   Activity: The Rules of the Game 64
5. **What Do You Value?** 69
   Activity: Identify Values 70
   Activity: Identify Core Principles 72
   Activity: Checking Alignment: Test Your Principles Against Your Why 74
   Activity: Identify Your Rules 76
6. **Vigorous Debate** 79
   Activity: Vigorous Debate 82

7. **Best Rule** 85
   Activity: The Best 88
   Activity: The Zig Rule 94
8. **The Commitment Rule** 99
   Activity: Your Commitments 102
9. **The Celebrate Rule** 105
   Activity: Let's Celebrate! 107
10. **The Learning Rule** 111
    Activity: Learning Through Failure 113
11. **The Importance of Boundaries** 115
    Activity: Defining Boundaries 119
12. **Communicating Rules and Values** 123
13. **The Tell, Trust, Fail, Shame Box** 129
14. **Writing Your Story** 139
    Activity: Vivid Vision 141

Conclusion 145
Acknowledgments 147
About the Author 149

Foreword

When I was finished writing this guide, I knew I needed to find someone to write the foreword. I had a list of people that I was considering—several kind, thoughtful, and accomplished people. During this time, my editor, April Kelly, was interviewing several clients of mine to get a feel for how their coaching experience was.

When April sent me these interviews, I was blown away reading about the impact coaching had on them. Frankly, in some ways I regret not knowing the impact for so long—some of these clients have been with me for two years now. And I know it sounds cliché, but I was so humbled by what they said. After reading through the interviews, it became clear to me who should write my foreword—my clients. This book wouldn't exist without them, after all.

My hope is that anyone who reads this book and implements what they learn will experience the same impact.

> "Most business books are stories about how the CEO is such an amazing leader, and their company is thriving, and if you do everything the way they tell you to, you'll succeed. Reading Lloyd's book and finding vulnerable stories about all the times he broke his own rules, and the failure that came about as a result, and then the valuable lessons he learned from those situations was a breath of fresh air."

> "Lloyd has forced me to really think about things deeply as he helps me bring different aspects of the business into focus. He challenges me to go deeper and think of the larger picture, the bigger impact. Why I am doing what I'm doing. I've learned to be more intentional in my actions. Every scenario we go over comes back to my 'why.'"

—JOHN DAVID TERRY, 3923 MANAGEMENT

"… it was time to grow and improve. We knew we needed the right coach to do that. Without someone who had experience growing a business, we were just making it up as we went along. Having someone who has been through this process before challenges us. He asks questions nobody else would ask, questions no one would even think of asking. Lloyd keeps us accountable, and we trust him with that."

"It has really impacted our team as a whole. One of our employees told me, 'Now we really know what you want!' So we've been successful in communicating our vision with the team."

—JACOB MORENO, ALTURA ENGINEERING AND DESIGN

"I didn't expect to be able to talk to Lloyd about everything in my life, not just the business. Lloyd is a business owner and an entrepreneur, so he deeply understands our experiences and how they shape our lives. Because of that, we delve into all facets of life whether business or personal. He shares things he's done in his own life that have helped him, like improving his fitness. That's been really inspiring for me. Coaching has helped my business but also my personal life."

—DAVID SALAS, ALTURA ENGINEERING AND DESIGN

"Lloyd helped me specifically with something I was bad at. It was tied to the imposter syndrome that plagued me when I first started this position -- I used to say, 'we're going to try' or 'we hope'. People use the words 'try' or 'hope' to build in a gray area, and he's helped me to stop doing that. Before, picking a direction and committing to it was difficult for me. Now, if I'm not confidently moving forward I know there is a problem somewhere."

—BRIAN ENEVOLDSEN, WT ENTERPRISE CENTER

"Coaching with Lloyd has greatly impacted our hiring process. We've also learned to work with key employees in our business to help them grow, and help them become better at managing people and hiring people. We're learning to help our key employees become leaders in their own right who can help the business grow. Lloyd is actually coming in for our second quarter meeting to meet with our leadership team."

—COY MCKAY, TURKEY CREEK HDD

"Coaching with Lloyd has reduced my stress at work. Also, it's lit a fire under my whole team. Everyone knows where we're headed now and they're either on board, or they aren't. But there's no ambiguity now, people have been pulled out of their complacency."

—MARK GILBREATH, CAPROCK BUILDING SYSTEMS

Introduction

Why did I write this guide? That's as good a place as any to begin introducing you to the following pages. After my first book, *Refined by Failure*, was released, the number of clients I was coaching increased quite a bit. As I met with these CEOs and leaders, I realized that it would be helpful to have a series of videos to use as a companion to my coaching. Some guidance is unique to specific clients, but a lot of information applies to all of them, and it would be convenient to have it all in one place, in the order in which I would be using it.

I began this process on my own, writing out what I wanted to say and recording myself as I presented the information. After the first several videos, I found myself stagnating. I was procrastinating, putting off doing the things I needed to do. That's when I read *Who Not How*, by Dan Sullivan and Dr. Benjamin Hardy. Everyone should read this book, whether or not they are in a leadership role. The basic idea is that if you are having trouble with the "how" aspect of a project, you may need to start looking for "who" instead.

We all have strengths, and one of my strengths is in-person coaching and building relationships. I thought that skill could seamlessly translate into creating a video series, but I was wrong. Because script-writing isn't a skill of mine, my brain was responding by putting it off, feeling frustrated, and feeling bad about myself for procrastinating. You know, that voice that says, "You should be doing this," or "You should be doing that."

When you realize that a project's "how" isn't in your wheelhouse, you need to find a partner with the skill you need. When your ideas partner with someone who has the skills to bring them to life, there's a synergistic energy that just doesn't exist otherwise. You may be good at your skill when you work on your own, and they may be good at their skill, but when you come together with a shared vision—magic happens.

So I contacted April Kelly, one of the editors who helped me when I wrote my first book, and asked if she'd be interested in helping me create a script for a video series based on that book. She was thrilled to be a part of the continuation of that project and came on board immediately. What happened next? It blossomed. Content just poured out of me and April translated it into script material.

As we made our way to the end of the video scripts, we went over all of the content we created and she joked, "It's like we wrote another book!" And a lightbulb went off. We HAD written another book! We had written the perfect companion guide for *Refined by Failure*. What did we do at that point? We pivoted. April began revising scripts to book content, and we worked together to flesh out things that were supposed to have been jumping off points for coaching in the videos.

Writing this book was an unintended result of creating a video course. There are great blessings that come from unintended results.

This book is a collection of things I've learned through my clients in coaching sessions, from insights that came to me when pondering the content in my first book, and from really great teachers. My wish is that you can avoid making the mistakes I did, and most importantly, to become aware of areas in which you are not being intentional. If you don't live your life with intention, it simply moves forward with no real direction.

The greatest influence on this guide has been from Stephen MR Covey and Simon Sinek. It starts with "why" you want to lead, and then "how" you lead. Simon Sinek addresses how to find your why, while Stephen MR Covey helps you understand how to be a transformational leader as opposed to a commanding leader.

I'm so glad that I've had the opportunity to coach others, because I've found through the writing of this book that I have learned more through our coaching sessions than my clients have! There is a great quote about this phenomenon by Yogi Bhajan, "If you want to learn something, read about it. If you want to understand something, write about it. If you want to master something—teach it."

I want to encourage you not to hurry through this guide and the exercise contained within. These concepts can take time to really sink in, and it takes a lot of self-reflection to get the most out of this process. If you need to complete a chapter and then put the book down to process what you've learned, then do that. However you learn best, just make sure to be intentional about this.

CHAPTER 1

What is Your Story?

During the course of this book, we're going to go through a series of activities that reveal your true values, then look at why you value those things, and then how you live those values at work and at home. We are also going to identify failures, and redefine them as learning events.

If you haven't seen the introductory course, I want to welcome you. This book is meant to be a practical guide to living the principles outlined in my first book, *Refined by Failure*. To completely understand the process we're going to go through, it would be helpful to have read that book first. However, anyone can benefit from the information, activities, and self-discovery contained in this book.

This book and the principles within are about the process of being refined. My own experience started a process that I'm going to share with you on redefining **failure** as **learning**. For me, it was being fired that was the catalyst that revealed my challenges with relationships. I learned that most, if not all, of my relationship issues were caused by a lack of clarity.

I hope these revelations help you reframe your own failures as lessons, to help clarify how you lead.

My Story

As I mentioned before, this book is a practical guide to implementing the ideas from my first book, *Refined by Failure*. When I wrote that first book initially, that wasn't the title. My idea for the book had centered around outlining my 10 Rules for business, how they each came to be, what they meant to me, and how to implement them. Well, I started writing, and story after story just poured out of me and I realized as I read them—all of these stories were about how I DIDN'T follow my rules, and what happened as a result. I wasn't writing a how-to, I was writing a how-not-to. In doing some soul-searching it became clear to me that each of these "failures" refined me into the person I am today.

My failure to ask for help, to **trust** others, drove a wedge between me and my wife, to the point that she asked me point-blank if I was having an affair.

My failure to hold a dear friend and team member accountable to the 10 Rules, and my subsequent refusal to engage in **vigorous debate** about the issue, drove a wedge between me and my team.

My failure to create clarity in my **commitments** led to diminishing trust with my partners and my team.

Those are just a few examples of the valuable lessons I learned along my journey so far. They certainly aren't the only ones, and they certainly won't be my last. These failures damaged my relationships, and if you don't have strong relationships with your family and business partners, you don't have a strong foundation, which creates a shaky vision. This leaves your relationships open to doubt and fear. If they don't trust you, they'll doubt your word. This is the basis for Rule 1, Give Trust, Earn Trust.

What I learned from these failures:
- Give trust, earn trust, rather than giving blind trust.
- Define plans for both success and failure—not just success.
- Being a know-it-all is a weakness, not a strength.
- If you lead with only your words and not your actions, you're a hypocrite—and hypocrites are not trustworthy.

Our Relationship with Failure

My goal in walking you through the process of creating values, and redefining values, is to help you reduce shame and have less regret when you get to the end of your journey.
- Failure is not who you are, it's an event.
- Failure is part of the journey—not the end.
- Learning from both your failures and your successes is how you improve.

We learn through failure, as it reveals what we didn't know and gives us the lesson needed for our future success.

Let's start by slowing down and asking yourself: what do I need to stop, what am I doing right and need to repeat, and what needs to be adjusted?

One thing that has helped me tremendously in my journey has been the support of a mental coach. When you want to be a better leader, you hire a business coach, when you want to get fit, you hire a physical coach. How much more important is your own mind? That's where every action begins.

In addition to my mental coach, I've also utilized the Kolbe A Index. When you know how your mind works, not only can you work with it to improve your life, you can also understand why certain things don't "click" for you the way they seem to with other people. Part of clarity is knowing yourself as well as possible.

Activity: Write Your Story

The first big activity will be to write your own story. You might be wondering, "Why is this important? I'm here to learn how to be a better CEO, not write a book."

First, sometimes we can't fully understand the path our life has taken until we write it all out and look at the big picture. That's where we see the themes and overarching patterns we may not have noticed before.

And second, it's important for you to know that you really can write your own story. What do I mean by that? Think about this: **your story up till now has, in essence, written itself. Moving forward, you have the opportunity to write it yourself,** *intentionally*.

So dive in and be brutally honest. We will write a different story at the end of the course, and you will be able to see how your perspective has changed. You will benefit most from this book if you complete this exercise before moving forward. I know that life gets in the way and you may not be able to do that, and that's okay. Complete as much as you can, and come back to it as needed.

| ACTIVITY 1 | WRITING YOUR OWN STORY |

Before you write, open up a blank document, or a blank journal page to work through the following prompts.

First, think of any events in your life, both business and personal, that you identify as a failure and write them down.

Remember that no one but you will see this brain dump, so please be brutally honest with yourself.

After you've gathered these stories together, begin to work through this next section.

PART ONE

For this activity, either enter the text after the prompt, or, if you're handwriting your coursework, simply write out your answers on paper.

If there is someone you really care about that you would want to share your story with, what are the most important life lessons they should know?

What would you want them to understand about you? Why?

What one, big, overarching idea do you believe your life story conveys? Why?

PART TWO

What is your biggest regret?

Why?

What were the impacts on your business and personal life?

What was the cost?

List the benefits in your life.

Repeat the five questions above for any event in your life that you want to reframe, from "failure" to "life lesson."

PART THREE: THE STORIES

Take your answers to the questions in part two, and write out the stories associated with these events as a narrative. Pretend you're telling these stories to someone out loud. How would you express them? Tell them in whatever order makes the most sense to you, it doesn't have to be chronological. Write them in a way that illustrates the path your life has taken.

I've included some examples of this from *Refined by Failure*.

Learning to Incorporate the Possibility of Failure When You Make a Commitment
"One million dollars!"

I was hoping I'd heard him wrong.

"The forecast wasn't accurate." The panic emanating from my CFO was palpable. "I didn't account for all the franchise taxes we'll have to pay."

I knew what he was going to say next before the words left his mouth.

"Lloyd, we're not going to be able to make our numbers."

The words hit me like a punch to the gut. Only the month before, I'd promised our partners a large equity distribution, and negotiated bonuses for myself and the team. The board had already approved and paid out that money in good faith, based on the last financial report from our CFO.

My credibility with the board was already in question based on the underperformance of the Mid-Continent Group, and this was just one more straw on the camel's already strained back.

You Are Not A Lone Wolf
This should have been one of the happiest moments of my life, but I felt numb and empty. I had just closed on the $60-million sale of my company to a private equity group, and that evening there was an impromptu celebration with my—now former—partners...

The next morning was no improvement when my CFO, Jim, burst into my office. "Lloyd, we're out of money! When the investors closed, they didn't leave us any capital to operate with and we'll need to make a draw on our line of credit. Payroll is due tomorrow."

Shock turned to dismay as I let out a heavy sigh. "OK. Let's get on the phone with the new bank and see if we can get some cash in the account."

You see, I had re-invested 80 percent of the cash from the sale back into the new partnership. The new partners had emphasized the importance of showing the investors that our management team was committed to the company, and this was especially true for me. To appease them and close the deal, I committed more resources than any of the other managing partners. I'd done this on my own, thinking it was the right decision, without first asking my wife or any other trusted advisors for their input. Then, there we were, already looking at being out of compliance with our new bank...

How was I going to tell my wife that I was going to lose 80 percent of the money from the sale of the company and just as important, what I'd spent the last twelve years building? All the time spent away from both her and my daughter, consumed with the business and nothing to show for it!

How would she respond? Would she forgive me?

The Problem With Sacred Cows

Have you created sacred cows in your life? People or decisions that cannot be questioned? This may be something to evaluate.

I was 17 when a blizzard hit our town, and when the Red Cross asked for volunteers with four-wheel-drive, it sounded like the perfect excuse to take my GMC Jimmy on a joy ride through the snow. As I rolled in, ready to help rescue stranded families and brave the elements, I started to see myself as a bit of a hero. That's when I met Jay, the Volunteer Commander of the local Red Cross. He was in his element: cool under pressure, able to see the whole picture, develop a plan, then calmly and clearly distribute orders to the eager, but inexperienced, volunteers running around the parking lot.

These same qualities would, many years later, make Jay an excellent executive to have in a crisis.

After many years of friendship and trust, Jay was my first choice when I needed to bring in a new VP of Environmental Health and Safety. Whenever a crisis hit, it was like being back in that blizzard. Jay was stoic, like the captain of a ship; he stayed focused on getting us through the storm. His orders came quickly, without any excess emotion, until the crisis was over.

This made him an invaluable asset during a crisis, when every second counts.

However, for most businesses the goal is to minimize the number of crises you have to face as an organization. This meant that for the vast majority of any given year, the same characteristics that made him such a great leader in a crisis, made him a difficult leader to work with outside of those circumstances.

I knew this intellectually, but would often find myself defending the tradeoff as worth it, because on the rare occasion we did have issues, I knew I could trust him to handle it.

It wasn't until I started reviewing his team evals that I started to recognize I had a problem.

Now write an outline using the rules that you live by. I used my 10 Rules as my outline, as you can see from the book. You can use them as an outline for your own, or if you have a set of rules or guidelines you live by, that's a great place to start. You can organize your stories based on these rules, OR, if you don't have rules, your stories may help you see what you may need to implement in your life.

I've included my original book outline[1] in the course materials for reference if you need some inspiration.

Below you'll find an outline template that you can use as a jumping off point. If you have more than four stories, feel free to keep going!

Your Outline

STORY 1

1. Opening
2. The story
3. What was the decision?
4. How did it go wrong?
5. How did it end?

STORY 2

1. Opening
2. The story
3. What was the decision?
4. How did it go wrong?
5. How did it end?

STORY 3

1. Opening
2. The story
3. What was the decision?
4. How did it go wrong?
5. How did it end?

---

[1] https://drive.google.com/file/d/1GSCEFs3SA1OOGzCEiZ7kl1t767t7ViY7/view?usp=sharing

STORY 4

1. Opening
2. The story
3. What was the decision?
4. How did it go wrong?
5. How did it end?

How Failure Impacts Our Decisions

I hope you were able to complete the "Writing your Story" activity. I can't tell you the revelations I had about myself when I began to write my own story, I mean REALLY write my own story, the good and the bad, not just the parts that made me look perfect.

What were the failures you identified when writing out your own story? Are there any that you ended up using as a learning opportunity?

I definitely had a moment like that in my journey. At Smart Chemical, we always said rule #1 was the safety rule and that people mattered, but we weren't practicing that.

One morning I woke to a call telling me our crew had a car accident. Our driver had fallen asleep at the wheel en route to the job site that morning but had miraculously woken up at the last minute, barely swerving away in time to avoid a head-on collision. Had he not woken up when he did, he would have driven into the oncoming tractor trailer, likely killing everyone on board.

When I heard this recounting, I was immediately transported back to my dad's funeral, thinking about the hundreds of people in attendance. Quickly doing the math in my head I realized that our crew of four, plus the driver, could have easily represented almost two thousand lives impacted by their deaths.

That was the impetus for changes made. One of which was that I would attend each new employee orientation. I needed to know each person to remind myself how much it mattered to honor rule #1. The wreck, remembering how I felt when my dad died, and thinking about how their families would feel if someone passed away—that's what changed everything.

When we make decisions and take action that ends up failing, it doesn't just affect that situation, it affects future decisions as well. In this case, that failure impacted future decisions in a positive way, but that's not always the case.

An important distinction to make is to ask: Am I failing due to a mistake or just a lack of competency? I had a client recently who was feeling like a failure because he had to let someone go. This was a person who had worked for him for nine years and he felt like he didn't handle it correctly. I asked him, "How many times have you had to fire someone who had worked for you for that many years?" His answer was, "Never." You see, he felt like a failure even though he was doing something he had never done before. When he looked at it that way, he realized he actually did a great job considering he had no experience. We do that to ourselves all the time, criticize ourselves for things we've never done.

When you first started riding a bike, it was new. When you were very little you probably didn't even know what a bike was. Then you saw the kids in the neighborhood riding their bikes and asked your parents to teach you. They bought you training wheels, and you got really good at riding with training wheels. Then you decided you wanted to learn to ride without them, and they taught you how to do that. Over time, you became unconsciously competent. That means, you knew how to ride that bike without thinking. You could make decisions about bike riding based on your competence and not fear from past failures. But what about back when you were first learning and weren't yet competent? If you fell, that would absolutely affect your decisions the next time you got on the bike.

> **Ask yourself:** *Am I making decisions based on self-awareness? Or am I making decisions that are influenced by my shame from my past failures?*

Exercise: I would encourage you to make a list of decisions in your life, whether they were made with awareness, or made based on past failures. Would those situations have turned out differently if you had made the decision based on your current reality at the time? Are you being overly critical because you expected results when you weren't fully competent? How would you avoid that in the future? Learn to know the difference between a bad decision and a lack of knowledge by completing the next activity.

ACTIVITY 2 — EVALUATING YOUR DECISIONS

Make a List

Make a list of decisions in your life, and consider the following questions:
- Was this decision made with awareness? What I mean by that is, did you make this decision based on past failures? Being aware of your past failures is good, as long as you don't allow your view to be influenced by shame. Did you make the decision because it was comfortable—what you were used to doing—or did you analyze your past failures WITHOUT SHAME and choose a different path based on what you learned?
- What would have turned out differently in this situation if you had objectively assessed past failures first?
- How are you being overly critical because you expected results when you weren't fully competent?
- Reflecting on your answers above, how would you avoid that and/or change your decisions in the future? Learn to know the difference between a bad decision and a lack of knowledge.

My List

1.

2.

3.

4.

5.

6.

7.

8.

9.

10.

You Are Not Alone

As humans, we tend to believe our experiences are unique, especially our failures. But the truth is we have all made bad decisions, whether they were made out of fear, ignorance, lack of competence, or simply wanting to do something on our own without help from trusted friends and partners.

As a CEO, it is important—no, vital—that you have trusted advisors you can go to when you need to work through a problem.

When I learned that I was being asked to step down as the CEO of Smart Chemical, my first thought was "I can't tell my wife!" and my second thought was "I feel so alone." After getting that news, I was numb and in shock. At that point, I decided to call my coach, Mike, from [CEO Coaching International](https://ceocoachinginternational.com/)[2]. Of course, he gave me great advice: I needed to tell Lora. Then he shared that he had been through something similar, that he would help me walk through this, and that eventually it would be okay.

After talking to Mike, I called my best friend Kurt, who is also my pastor. He confirmed everything Mike had advised and said that we would make it together. That evening when I got home, Lora had made dinner. I waited until after we ate to tell her the news. In true Lora fashion, she took a moment to gather her thoughts before reassuring me that we would get through this together.

I no longer felt alone!

Choosing the right Trusted Advisor(s) is so critical. Who are your advisors? Are they effective in your life? I would encourage you to complete the activity, Choosing a Trusted Advisor, to evaluate who is helping you make decisions.

---

[2] https://ceocoachinginternational.com/

| ACTIVITY 3 | CHOOSING A TRUSTED ADVISOR |

Who makes a good advisor, and who does not? The answer might surprise you. Most people think of their family and friends when it comes to advice. However, family, friends, investors, and employees are not good Trusted Advisors because they each have an emotional or financial connection to you and your decisions.

Other CEOs from peer groups like Vistage, CEO Coaching International, Strategic Coach, or YPO (Young Presidents' Organization), or any other local or online CEO peer group or coaching group you may be a part of are the best choices. These are people who understand your day-to-day life in a way no one else does, and they're unbiased since they have no stake in your decisions.

Use this sheet to list people you already go to for advice. What is your relationship with them? How trustworthy are they? Based on those answers, are they a good Trusted Advisor? Next, list people who you believe could become advisors in your life.

PERSON	RELATIONSHIP	TRUST	GOOD ADVISOR
Ex. Joe Carpenter	A colleague from my local CEO peer group	Yes	Yes
Ex. Tom Davis	A fellow CEO, and a friend I've known since I was 12	Yes	No

28 | REFINING THROUGH FAILURE *THE GUIDE*

Be Refined, Not Defined, by Failure

Failure is part of the journey—not the end. Slow down and ask yourself: what do I need to stop, what did I do right and need to repeat, and what do I need to adjust? Learning from both your failures and your successes is how you improve.

Some of the best lessons in my life were also the most painful. My first divorce taught me a lot about what I don't want in personal relationships. Being fired as the CEO of Smart Chemical showed me what I shouldn't do as a leader. Those were two of the best learning times of my life.

The biggest part of learning is not to wallow in shame. Accept responsibility for what you can change and let go of what you cannot. Remember that guilt is a good thing because it tells us that we need to make a change, but shame is not because it defines you by the failure. It's self-focused rather than being focused on change. It makes you define yourself by what went wrong rather than who you are as a person in that situation.

What's The Point?

Failure is part of the journey—not the end. Are you identifying with the shame and allowing it to negatively influence decisions? Or are you learning through failure?

Takeaway

Slow down and ask yourself: what do I need to stop, what am I doing right and need to continue, and what needs adjustment? Learning from both your failures and your successes is how you improve.

Resources

- *Refined by Failure*, C. Lloyd Brown
- CEO Coaching International – www.ceocoachinginternational.com
- Vistage – www.vistage.com
- Strategic Coach – www.strategiccoach.com
- Young Presidents' Organization (YPO) – www.ypo.org

CHAPTER 2

Why We Do What We Do

Before you begin this chapter, I'd like to invite you to watch a powerful TED Talk by Simon Sinek[1] on how your "Why" impacts your life.

After you watch the video, I would like to take you through what's called the "I AM" process. Do you know who you are outside of what you do? Many people define themselves solely based on what they do, and never take the time to discover who they ARE.

You can't get to your why without first understanding who you are, and how to discover that.

One way I've explored who I am is by utilizing personality and aptitude tests such as 16 Personalities and the Kolbe A index. While 16 Personalities is more about who you are and how you behave, Kolbe A evaluates how you learn and how you work best. I'd encourage you to explore both of them to help you better understand yourself.

The I AM process can be uncomfortable, because it helps reveal negative I AM statements. These are your shame areas. "I am stupid" "I am lazy" "I am ..." We live up or down to our expectations. Working with my "mental coach" has done so much to help me understand the source of the negative statements and reveal the positive identity over the negative.

Your why stems from your identity, who you identify yourself as. You have an identity, even if you don't realize what it is.

My own personal belief was "I AM a know it all and I don't need anyone to help me make decisions." This was an unhealthy I AM statement which came from my beliefs about what others expected from me. I believed they expected me to have all the answers, and I had to BS my way through many situations because of that expectation. For most of my life, I struggled with being a people pleaser.

I suffered from a lack of awareness, and because of this I didn't realize that was my identity. I was lying to myself and others but wasn't aware of that fact. I made many promises to change over the years, but the changes never lasted. My true desire was to change, but without understanding "why" I

---

[1] If you're reading a physical copy of this book, simply go to YouTube and search "Simon Sinek Why" and it will be one of the first results.

made decisions the way I did, there was no way to change because we DO what we BELIEVE. Until we know our "why" we can never truly change.

Until you know your WHY, you can never truly change!

When **what you do and what you say don't match**, that reveals hypocrisy, and trust is lost. Then you become like those old Godzilla movies, where your face is moving one way, but your words don't match up. For you younger folks, think about English-dubbed Japanese anime. Their mouths don't always match the words you're hearing.

By discovering your why, you can see who you really are and live life with awareness.

What do you think your why is currently?

What are your beliefs?

Do your actions reveal those beliefs?

If not, what beliefs do your actions display?

Your true why (5 whys in) will motivate people to want to join you and support you. It creates clarity so no one can question your motives—that lack of clarity invites fear. When there is a lack of clarity, there will be a lack of trust.

A good mental coach is also a great resource in helping you uncover your why. They're completely unbiased and able to help you work through your internal beliefs without judgment.

First, we'll do an activity to help you identify who you believe you are. Then, in the next section, we'll explore how to find your WHY.

| ACTIVITY 1 | "I AM" |

After you've watched Simon Sinek's TED Talk, practice writing out all of your "I AM" belief statements.

Identify both your positive reinforcing statements as well as the negative ones and evaluate how they impact your decisions. There may also be neutral statements. Think about those and evaluate how they make you feel about yourself. Neutral statements lack passion.

Some examples from my own process are.

POSITIVE

- I am a child of God
- I am a good father
- I am a good husband

NEGATIVE

- I am stupid
- I am thoughtless

NEUTRAL

- I am a mediocre person

Summary

Mediocre I AM statements have no passion. Negative statements drive decisions based on fear. Positive statements drive faith and give purpose.

Your Turn!

STATEMENT	POSITIVE NEGATIVE NEUTRAL	HOW DOES THIS BELIEF IMPACT MY DECISIONS?
Ex. I am a good father	Positive	This belief sets the standard for my relationship with my child, and if I'm tempted to lose my temper or act in a way that I wouldn't consider being a "good father" it helps me stop and reevaluate what I'm doing.
Ex. I am stupid	Negative	When I approach any situation, I automatically believe I won't be able to do it right, which causes me not to make a commitment and/or dare to be great. Even worse than quitting, it can cause me not to even try.
Ex. I am an adequate leader	Neutral	This belief simply allows me to live up (or down) to a low expectation. I don't feel inspired to be better or do better because I feel "ok" about the situation. There is no passion or excitement in my leadership and it creates partners who are not passionate.

STATEMENT	POSITIVE NEGATIVE NEUTRAL	HOW DOES THIS BELIEF IMPACT MY DECISIONS?

Identifying Passion

Passion and Determination = Why

I met Garth several years ago when he was remodeling an old building, and my company was thinking about relocating into that building. After discussing it with Garth and gaining an understanding of what the situation would look like, I thought it was a good decision—and since Garth seemed like a trustworthy person, we agreed to a 5-year lease on a handshake.

One of my commitments after I was fired was to negotiate a rent abatement in order to make sure the company survived financially. When I called Garth, he immediately wanted to know how I was doing. I told him I was ok, but that I was calling to try and negotiate a rent abatement. Garth said of course, whatever you need—I will see what I can do. He ended up making the adjustments and ultimately helped the company survive.

He then asked me to lunch. We'd gone to lunch many times over the years. Garth was always generous with his time. Later, at his funeral, I learned there were many people he had touched with his willingness to listen. There were 1500 people at his funeral, and all had stories about Garth that were much like mine.

One story stood out among the rest, though. Garth was a car guy, and he owned a 1989 Toyota Land Cruiser that he had restored. Instead of keeping it at home, he kept this car at his office. One night, someone broke into the office, stole his keys, and took the car. The person was clearly under the influence, because they crashed through the garage door, took a wild ride around town crashing into many other things, and ended up running the car into his own home. When Garth learned about the theft, he asked, "Has the man been arrested?" When his employee told him that he had been, he instructed him to go get $1000 and take it to the man's wife, because her breadwinner was now in jail. Wow. That is true compassion and generosity.

My experiences with Garth truly illustrated how people will always remember how you treated them. I and many others at his funeral would have given anything just to have one more day with Garth. That's when my "why" began to take shape.

My Why: To be a person of influence, not position, and help others achieve their goals so at the end of my life God will say to me, "Well done my good and faithful servant," and that people who know me would wish they had just one more day.

I put that into action by learning to listen. And then listen again. And sometimes ONLY listen rather than responding. I don't know it all, and I don't have to, that's not what helps others.

Determining your why ties back to learning how you identify yourself.

My Why Statement

My why statement is made up of three distinct sections.

Part one is: "To be a person of influence, not position." This is the basis for the rest of the statement. If I focused on being a person of position, I wouldn't be able to connect with others in order to help them.

Which leads to part two: "Helping others achieve their goals so at the end of my life, God will say to me, 'Well done my good and faithful servant.'"

It was after the death of my friend Garth, and reflecting on my father's death, that I finished my why statement with the third part. I realized it was very important to me that when my time comes, "People who know me would wish they had just one more day."

My part three is a direct result of parts one and two, it's the scorecard, so to speak. If I succeed in living out the first two sections of my why, the third will naturally come to pass.

Now, I didn't just go through my 5 whys and immediately come up with this statement. In fact, it evolved over the course of about 16 months. I didn't even do it alone—my mental coach helped me work through what was most important to me. Remember, a strong heart requires a strong mind, and a mind coach helps you get there. Your spouse can't be your mental coach, nor your friend, you need someone who is neutral. Having a counselor is part of self-discovery.

Your Why Worksheet

Let's do some brainstorming.

First, your why isn't going to be based on any concepts that aren't already present in your life. You are who God made you to be. The easiest way to begin finding your why is to look back on your life so far, and focus on experiences where you were your best. Focus on positive themes that are present in your life.

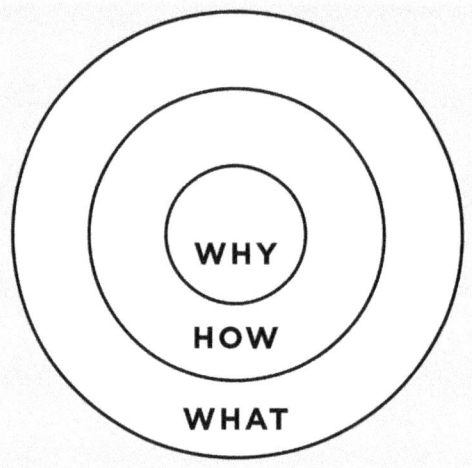

Figure 1. From Simon Sinek, *Start With Why*, Chapter 3

For example, maybe you are the person who always tries to help people look on the bright side—you see the glass as half-full rather than half-empty. That means that one of your natural traits is optimism. If it is one of your defining traits, it might be a component of your why statement.

Take a moment to jot down stories about where you were at your very best, doing things that made you feel happy and alive.

Identify common themes that run through these experiences.

Now think about what you want in life, and begin to ask yourself why.

Here was my "why" process when I started coaching, as an example:

Why are you coaching business leaders?
I want them to know that they're not alone. That there are resources and other leaders that want authentic relationships, and they will encourage them and become their friends.

Why?
Because business leaders are expected to know it all, or at least that's what we think, and I want to show how that thinking is flawed and is a real weakness for leaders.

Why?
Because we only have one life to live, and time is our greatest resource. Without understanding the value of our time, we make decisions that we feel we can fix later instead of doing it today, and that mentality wastes everyone's time—our time, our team members' time, and our stakeholders' time, and I want to help avoid that.

Why?
Because there is no way to time travel and get that time back. Most of my regret is around relationships that are lost or have been damaged because I did not value everyone's time and create personal boundaries that valued these relationships.

WHY are relationships important?
When I worked on my answer to that question, it was then that I realized that my real purpose in life is helping others.

Once your WHY begins to take shape, you'll put it into this format: To (insert contribution to the world) so that (what impact you'll have).

In Simon Sinek's book, *Start With Why*, he explains: "The first blank represents the contribution you make to the lives of others. The second blank represents the impact of your contribution."

Your first draft will probably be a very broad statement, something like "To be a good person so that people will love me." That statement is a nice goal, but there is nothing actionable. Nothing is defined. What is "good" to you? Who do you want to love you? What do you mean when you say "love"? If your why statement generates more questions than answers, it should definitely be refined further.

Simon Sinek's why statement reads: "To inspire people to do the things that inspire them so that, together, we can change our world."

His coauthor, David Mead, identified this as his why: "To propel people forward so that they can make their mark on the world."

Your Five Why Process

Start with what you want to do or be known for in life.

Why?

Why?

Why?

Why?

Why?

In light of the previous answers to "why," write part one of your why statement. Who do you need to be to accomplish the life you want to live?

Part two, what is it that you want to accomplish that rests on being that person?

Part three, what is the scorecard, so to speak? What do you want to happen at the end of your life to reflect that you've lived your why?

Now put it all together and write your WHY statement:

NOW... HOW?

Remember the image at the beginning of this worksheet? Having a why is great, but without a how, nothing will happen. Right now, just think about "how" and write down what comes to you. In the last exercise in this module, we'll turn these into actionable statements.

"How" oftentimes involves the important relationships in your life.

How will you implement your why into your personal relationships?

How will you implement your why into your business relationships?

What We Do

Determination = Obstacles don't stand in your way

Now that we've identified positive and negative statements and begun the journey to finding our WHY in the activities above, we're clear on who we are and why we do what we do.

This gives us the energy, stamina, and determination to live our lives. It allows us to identify what we can take action on that we are in control of, as well as identify what we're not in control of, and be able to let that go. We're now focused on and working toward our purpose rather than being held back by our fear of failure and/or lack of resources.

The next step is to share that why and purpose with others.

The following is an activity designed to help you write your own script to share with the people in your own life. Having this clear in your mind helps you not only to communicate it, but also to live it. This is important, and will prepare you for Chapter 4.

| ACTIVITY 3 | PERSONAL BELIEF SCRIPT |

Turning your WHY into a script to share with people in your life

Now that you've identified your I AM and WHY, write out a script that will help you understand how you're going to share your WHY with your family and trusted advisors, based on your why statement. Having this clear in your mind will help you communicate and live this. This script will be a big part of Chapter 4.

LLOYD'S SCRIPT

The following is my why process that I shared with you in the previous activity. Use this to help you if you haven't yet created your own:

Lloyd, Why are you coaching business leaders?
I want them to know that they're not alone. That there are resources and other leaders that want authentic relationships, and they will encourage them and become their friends.

Why?
Because business leaders are expected to know it all, or at least that's what we think, and I want to show how that thinking is flawed and is a real weakness for leaders.

Why?
Because we only have one life to live and time is our greatest resource. Without understanding the value of our time, we make decisions that we feel we can fix later instead of doing it today, and that mentality wastes everyone's time, our time, the employees' time, and our stakeholders' time.

WHY?
Because there is no way to time travel and get that time back. Most of my regret is around relationships that are lost or have been damaged because I did not value everyone's time and create personal boundaries that valued these relationships.

WHY are relationships important?
I realized that my real purpose in life is helping others.
    So, it became clear what my "Why" is for the rest of my life.
    I want to be a person of influence, not position, helping others achieve their goals so that at the end of my life, God says well done, good and faithful servant.

MY SCRIPT

Now follow the WHY process, as I did above, for your specific situation. My example above is my overarching, broad WHY for my life. But for each area you're serving, you should create the same clarity. You can use this to create scripts for every situation. Use the WHY's for your life in general, use it for your role in your family, use it for your role in your business, and so on.

How We Do It

Now that you know your why, how does that help you know how to move forward?

My why gave me clarity on what to say yes to, and what to say no to. It gave me energy and purpose. At the end of every day, I can now go back and look at where I was successful in living out my why, and the areas where I wasn't fulfilled, that didn't align with my why.

Living your why is like having a great meal: you're full but not stuffed—you're satisfied and content. You're looking forward to tomorrow—to getting to do it again. Exhausted but still fulfilled, knowing you'll wake up the next day energized. The alternative is to be exhausted but unfulfilled, creating turmoil. You're drained. You can't rest. There's nothing left in the tank and you don't even know if you can put anything in the tank. You lose your sense of wellbeing. If you go against your why you can't help people. You hit the wall. You can't go any further the way things are currently.

If your why is not defined, the things that you're doing are going to be defined by the why of the moment, not the why of your life.

Ultimately all the other chapters will be spent clarifying what we've talked about in this one. The remainder of this book rests on the foundation of this one chapter. My why is what evolved into my rules: Vigorous Debate, Celebrate, Safety, and so on. You'll use this to create your own rules. There is an activity on the next page, and the more work you put into it, the more valuable the rest of this book will be.

| ACTIVITY 4 | YOUR PERSONAL BELIEF MATRIX |

Write Your Matrix

For this exercise, it will be helpful to look back on the exercise, Start with Why. This takes your "how" questions and makes them actionable in your life.

Why Statement

How will you implement this in your life?

What actions will you take?

When will you start?

Where in your life do you need to implement these actions?

Who is a help to help you, and who may be hindering your journey? Sometimes you'll find there are people who keep you from living your why, and there are others whose support makes living your why easier.

What's The Point?
Your why stems from your identity, who you identify yourself as. If you don't define your identity, you'll allow others to define it for you—thereby defining your why.

Takeaway
If your why is not defined, what you do and how you accomplish the responsibilities related to your roles—they are going to be defined by the moment, instead of being purposeful and intentional.

Resources
- *Start with Why*, Simon Sinek
- Start with Why, How Great Leaders Inspire Action

CHAPTER 3

How Relationships Impact Your Life

How do you build a relationship based on trust? More importantly, how do you build trusting business relationships, allowing your company's goods or services to provide a value and/or a kept promise that creates a long-term relationship? Unless you are providing something unique, your company's product or service only brings value if people trust you—or if not you, they at least trust your commodity. Otherwise price will always be the final determining factor. That reduces you to the role of a vendor, versus being a partner.

It's that way with our personal relationships too. Without trust, you may just be a roommate versus a spouse or friend.

Without trust, you may be simply an authority figure for your children rather than a parent.

The same model works in every relationship you'll have in your life.

Relationships are defined and measured by whether or not we made, defined, and kept our commitments. Good relationships are based on kept commitments. When you make a commitment, you're saying that you will put forth your best effort and that you will follow through on your commitment. You plan for success, create contingencies for failure, and establish timelines for everyone involved to review the plan and how they'll keep their commitment.

Defining Relationships in Your Life

On a day-to-day basis, we don't usually actively define relationships in our lives. John may be your friend, but he may also be your business partner. He may also be your brother-in-law! The relationships in our lives can come with many labels and classifications. Those classifications come with different levels of commitment.

We subconsciously prioritize our relationships every day, and not always in the ways we should. Let's say Robert, your business partner, wants to meet on Friday night for dinner to discuss an important business matter. But your wife said yesterday that she misses spending quality time together and suggested you go out to dinner Friday night. Business is important, but you have already decided that your family takes precedence, and you ask Robert if the two of you can meet for breakfast that day instead.

However, maybe you haven't taken the time to think about your commitments to your family and you aren't making decisions based on their importance in your life, you only see the immediate problem — the business matter. You take the dinner with Robert, cancel with your wife, and break trust with her.

If you had taken the time to define the relationships in your life, it would have been easy to know what to say yes to, and what to say no to. Have you taken the time to define the relationships in your life and how to set boundaries and/or define commitments for each one?

Customer Relationships

Mike was a long-time customer of mine. He ran a division of a company called Magellan Midstream Partners, which owns and operates the largest network of refined petroleum products pipelines in the United States. My old company was his division supplier.

Mike had been working with some of my team members as a customer of my previous company since the late 1980s when I started Smart Chemical in 2008. Those three team members joined me at Smart in late 2009. I had a long-time relationship with Mike as well. We started as business associates but became great friends through our passion for hunting as well as our faith journeys. Because of these long-term, high-trust relationships, Mike offered to help get Smart on the bid list for Magellan and compete with our—much larger—old company. You see, our old company had made some pretty serious missteps after those teammates had left and Magellan was going to make a change.

There was a snag, though. Because there were nondisclosure agreements tied to our old company's technology, we were unable to use this knowledge and experience. If we were going to successfully acquire the Magellan business, we had to develop a completely new program. This spurred us to innovate new technology, rigorously test it, provide samples for third-party testing, and then provide it at a price to win. We had only 90 days to accomplish what normally is an 18-month process. Amazingly, we won. The relationship the four of us had with Mike was the foundation that set us on a path of rapid growth and development.

Financial Stakeholder Relationships

There are so many examples of times when a lack of communication and commitment with my financial stakeholders caused problems for me. I had these problems because I never fully defined those commitments.

For example, there was a time when my failure to plan for all outcomes caused me to lose trust with my team. You see, I'd promised our partners a large equity distribution after a sale, and negotiated bonuses for myself and the team. The board had already approved and paid out that money in good faith, based on the last financial report from our CFO. Unfortunately, it turned out that my CFO had miscalculated the franchise tax we would have to pay and, let's just say, it was enough that we were in the red after paying out the bonuses.

I made a commitment without fully exploring the scope of what I was committing to, and what would happen if any part of the plan fell through. Those relationships suffered as a result.

Employee Relationships

Jim was a team member of mine who had broken trust by falsifying inventory records. When doing routine reconciliation, the company found they were missing *tens of thousands of dollars of chemicals*. As they were going through that process, I was truly bewildered. I had really enjoyed working with Jim, and this seemed very out of character for him. That's when I decided there must be more to this story.

In thinking over the past year or so, I realized he had been under a lot of responsibility—managing a warehouse while also delivering inventory. Because I was requiring so much of his time, he felt he needed to take a shortcut. As we went through counseling with Jim, I found he'd basically been 'pencil whipping' the inventory report, basing the numbers on what he thought they probably were. That means he wasn't following our standard processes—he had experienced something called the 'normalization of deviation' (more on that in Chapter 14). He had essentially stopped going through every part of the checklist. Because he had always had a good attitude, and had been a good team member, we suspended him for a week without pay, then brought him back.

He thrived in the role and even after I left, he continued to be promoted within that organization and is now a high-level manager there. While he'd had a good attitude before, he came back with an even better attitude. He took the opportunity to learn, rather than wallow in what was a pretty serious failure. We both learned through this process and were ultimately blessed and have a good relationship to this day.

There are several important components to this story, concepts that we will dig into as we go along:

- The failure was a direct result of not following established processes (chapter 14).
- Jim said 'yes' to everything we asked of him in an attempt to placate leadership, even though he should have been honest about his ability to manage so much (chapter 9).
- We did not consider Jim's competency level when adding responsibilities (chapter 7).
- Jim didn't allow the failure to define him, he learned from it.
- Though he did break trust, he put in the effort to rebuild that trust successfully (chapter 12).
- Jim's good attitude is what we looked at when deciding how to proceed. We knew that someone with a good attitude and a willingness to learn was an asset (chapter 7).

Make Sure Your Employees Know You Care

In my goal to connect with each employee during my time as CEO, my assistant would bring me a stack of cards at the beginning of each month, one for each employee's birthday. I personally filled them out, writing a message to each one. That one small thing let everyone know that I knew who they were, and I remembered their birthday. That's rare for a CEO with 200+ employees. That small act of intention reflects the golden rule in that relationship.

Family and Friend Relationships

LORA

I walked in the door one day after fishing with a friend to find Lora standing in front of me. She told me she was done. I wasn't sure what she was done with so I didn't know how I should respond. Then she continued, telling me she was serious, and asked me if I'd read Dave Hollis's book *Get Out Of Your Own Way* like I'd agreed to.

Thankfully I had. She had too, and she realized that her own life was blowing around in the breeze just like mine, because we were a team, and my decisions affected her.

I had made many promises to change over the years, but the changes never lasted. My true desire was to change, but without understanding "why" I made decisions the way I did, there was no way to change. It wasn't until I went through the WHY process that I was able to make the necessary changes, by the way.

I decided that first I would admit that I was a "Know It All." Second, I would work on my mind—as Dave said in his book, "Working out a muscle in your arm doesn't imply you had bad arms before they were strong, but for some reason digging into why we do the things we do, how we're motivated, our habits, what we focus on—that work seems to call into question something at our core that defines us as either strong or weak, fit for more or destined for less, born with it or not."

Thankfully I made the changes in my life that have had a positive effect on our relationship and our life together.

JAY

At 17 years old, I met Jay. He was larger than life and became a mentor to me. After many years of friendship and trust, Jay was my first choice when I needed to bring in a new VP of Environmental Health and Safety. Whenever a crisis hit, Jay was stoic, like the captain of a ship; he stayed focused on getting us through the storm. His orders came quickly, without any excess emotion, until the crisis was over.

This made him an invaluable asset during a crisis, when every second counts. It did not make him an asset in the day-to-day workings of running a business. He was gruff and didn't think about how his words and actions came across to others.

You see, I knew this about Jay, but I didn't set boundaries in the beginning of our working relationship. My lack of clarity in the beginning allowed conflict to happen. How could Jay know what appropriate behavior was in our workplace if I didn't define it? How could he have known he would be fired for that behavior if I had never defined that?

In the end, my failure forced me to fire a mentor and dear friend—somebody who had been a protector, defender, and advocate for me—all because I didn't address his behaviors soon enough. It wasn't long after, on November 6, a mutual friend called and told me Jay had died, on his 69th birthday.

I had just been on the phone with him two hours earlier wishing him a happy birthday. He was in the bathroom of the DMV at the time, waiting to get his license and said he didn't feel very good. He was so happy to hear from me, nonetheless, and we talked for a few minutes before he said he needed to get back to the lobby, not wanting to miss his turn.

What I learned from our friend, Leonard, was that not long after talking to me, Jay had a massive heart attack and died. I was so sad; I'd lost someone who was always there for me.

The next activity is to identify those who help you live your purpose. You'll rank these relationships anywhere from 1-5, based on your level of commitment to this person, and how much influence they hold in your life.

| ACTIVITY 1 | DEFINE AND CLASSIFY KEY RELATIONSHIPS |

What kinds of relationships do you have in your life?

On a day-to-day basis, we don't usually actively identify relationships in our lives. John may be your friend, but he may also be your business partner. He may also be your brother-in-law! The relationships in our lives can come with many labels. Have you taken the time to identify the relationships in your life?

The People in My Life with Whom I Need to Have a Clear Understanding of Boundaries and Commitments

List the key relationships in your life. Your spouse, children, close family, investors, stakeholders, customers, employees, etc. Anyone who impacts how you live your purpose. List their name, all the relationships they have with you, and then classify the commitment they require in your life.

You can classify people as 1, 2, 3, 4, or 5. Your level 1 relationships are heart commitments: family, whether by blood or by choice. These are the people who are most important in your life and the people to whom your commitment is the highest. All decisions you make are filtered by whether or not that decision will prevent you from keeping your commitments to your level 1 relationships.

Your level 2 relationships are a combination of a heart commitment and a contract commitment, and are made up of friends, employer/employee relationships, investors, stakeholders, board members. Important people to whom you are committed, but who come second to your level 1 relationships.

Level 3 is a pure contractual commitment and consists of people like your customers, your banker, and other tertiary relationships that would come second to levels 1 and 2.

Level 4 would encompass acquaintances and people who are on the periphery of your world. They aren't people to whom you make many, or any, commitments, but may be connected to your life enough that your decisions may occasionally impact them.

Lastly, level 5 would be the people in the world around you, who don't necessarily impact your life.

Defining and classifying your relationships is important because the higher the importance of your relationship with someone, the higher your commitment to them is. The higher your commitment is to someone, the more important it is to define those commitments as well as boundaries.

You'll notice that the first example falls into two relationship categories. The highest level is the one that applies. Knowing when someone falls into two levels is important because that will impact how you make decisions and commitments with that person.

NAME	RELATIONSHIP	COMMITMENT LEVEL
John McHale	Brother, customer*	1
Jennifer Davis	Wife	1
Matthew Bedford	Investor, stakeholder	2
Judith Miles	Customer	3
Amy Martin	Banker	3
Joe	Barista at my coffee shop	4

What's The Point?
Relationships are measured by whether or not we made, defined, and kept our commitments.

Takeaway
If you don't take the time to define your relationships, you may end up prioritizing the wrong ones.

Resources
- *Refined by Failure*, C. Lloyd Brown
- *How Will You Measure Your Life*, Clayton M Christensen with James Allworth and Karen Dillon

CHAPTER 4

Defining Our Rules and Boundaries

Looking back to Chapter 2, remember I said it would be foundational for Chapter 4? Knowing and being firm and solid in your own WHY is the basis for your personal boundaries. Knowing your WHY will help you know what to say YES to, and when—and what to say NO to, and when. What in your life is in line with your WHY and what isn't? When someone asks you to do something you have to ask yourself: is this in line with my WHY?

Chapter 3 also helps us define boundaries because we've identified and classified the relationships in our lives, and the level of commitment to each.

Continually acting against your own why, and not having clarity on your relationships will wreak havoc with your life, because you will be making commitments haphazardly.

My 10 Rules

In my first book, *Refined by Failure*, these rules are listed from the last rule to the first rule. That's because I was following Stephen R. Covey's advice from *The 7 Habits of Highly Effective People* to begin with the end in mind. However, here, I'm going to share them with you in order to illustrate how the Core 4 rules impact the others.

My ten rules are based on my why.

MY WHY

To be a person of influence, not position, helping others achieve their goals so at the end of my life, God will say to me, "Well done my good and faithful servant," and that people who know me would wish they had just one more day.

#1 Trust Rule: Give trust, earn trust. You can't influence people without trust. You can't help people reach their goals if they don't trust you.

#2 Safety Rule: If you don't go home at night, nothing else matters. How can someone say yes to you if they don't feel safe? Fear paralyzes us. If someone doesn't feel safe with you emotionally, how can you be an influence in their life?

#3 Golden Rule: Treat others as you would like to be treated. When you treat others as they would like to be treated, they will always wish you had one more day.

#4 Profit First Rule: This is about being a good steward, and that is vital to being a person of influence. It also reflects honoring the investment of time and effort by your team, the resources of your investors, and the trust of your customer.

#5 Vigorous Debate Rule: How can you help people achieve their goals without evaluating them and understanding the consequences of both success and failure? The purpose of the core four rules is to create an environment of trust where we are comfortable with these types of conversations.

#6 Best Rule: Helping people define what their best really is, and then understand what is possible, is vital to helping them achieve their goals.

#7 Zig Rule: "Help others get what you want, and eventually you will get what you want." Helping people achieve their goals is LITERALLY the Zig rule.

#8 Commitment Rule: Keeping commitments is the foundation of trust, which safeguards relationships.

#9 Celebrate Rule: This is about enjoying the journey rather than just looking toward the destination. Research has shown that groups who practice regular celebration (positive rituals) create stronger bonds. One study not only "...demonstrated that rituals lead to social bonding, but also provided support for the hypothesis that emotional state—and more specifically positive affect—is related to feelings of social connectedness..." [Charles SJ, van Mulukom V, Brown JE, Watts F, Dunbar RIM, Farias M (2021) United on Sunday: The effects of secular rituals on social bonding and affect. PLoS ONE 16(1): e0242546. https://doi.org/10.1371/journal.pone.0242546]

Celebrating builds relationships and creates memories that last a lifetime.

#10 The Learning Rule: This is essential to trust and also key to vulnerability. People who are vulnerable can admit their mistakes, and if you can admit a mistake, you can learn from it. To learn best, first we must recognize that failure is an event, not a person, and not everything you do will be successful.

We need to be dedicated to learning from our mistakes, and teaching, so we and others don't do the same thing over and over expecting different results—which is the definition of insanity, and destroys trust. If people in your life know that you are humble and reflective when something has gone wrong, and they know that you will make it right and learn from it, that solidifies trust in your relationship. Looking to one another for accountability creates trusting relationships as well, because you give that person trust by admitting you've failed. When you give trust, you earn trust.

The Core 4: Why They Are Important, What I Am, and Who I Want to Be

THE TRUST RULE

Give trust, earn trust, something I learned from Stephen MR Covey's *The Speed of Trust*, is vital to relationships. If you trust someone, you will earn their trust in return. Trust is the basis for all good relationships, both personal and business.

The Trust Rule was inspired by the book *The Speed of Trust* by Stephen M. R. Covey.

THE SAFETY RULE

If you don't go home at night, nothing else matters. Every person in your life has people who love them, who would be heartbroken if anything happened to them. Treat them as you would your own family and keep them safe.

The Safety Rule was inspired by the loss of my dad when I was 20, and the far-reaching impact of that. It was reinforced by the almost-fatal car accident involving my team members.

THE GOLDEN RULE

Treat others the way you want to be treated. This creates interpersonal safety in relationships. When you feel safe in a relationship, you can build trust. Treating others with respect is the cornerstone of strong relationships.

The Golden Rule was derived from the book of Matthew:

Matthew 7:12 (TPT) "In everything you do, be careful to treat others in the same way you'd want them to treat you, for that is the essence of all the teachings of the Law and the Prophets."

THE PROFIT FIRST RULE

This is really "people first." That may seem counterintuitive, but think about this, if your company goes under because you put celebration above profits, your employees won't have much to celebrate in the unemployment office. Putting profits first is putting your employees first. Profit is what pays their salary and helps them care for their families. If you put profit first, you and your staff will always have something to celebrate.

The Profit First Rule was inspired by the book *Profit First* by Mike Michalowicz.

I'd like to build an analogy of the 10 rules for you. Think about a game. Any game. Basketball, chess, or if you're not into games, this can even be applied to being a musician in a band or orchestra. A game has ground rules that establish the playing field, WHAT we're playing, then the rules of gameplay which is HOW you play.

The core 4 establishes the playing field in this way:

Give trust, earn trust: we agree to play the game according to the rules and boundaries.

Safety rule: we'll play the game with rules that ensure safety, both emotional and physical. So we go home at the end of the night the way we were before the game started.

Golden rule: Play the game to strengthen each other, and continue to build trust.

Profit-first rule: Understanding how we keep score. In the game of business, that's how much profit we make. When we win, we have money to reinvest and continue to grow the business. And winning is fun.

Why and How I Practice the Core Values, Using the Other 6

Rules 5-10 are important, don't get me wrong, but they don't matter unless you have the core 4 as the foundation. If you don't have trust, you can't have vigorous debate. If you don't have the core 4 you can't understand what someone's best is.

Back to the game analogy, games have a time clock, boundaries so they know what is out of bounds, requirements for the size of the field, etc.—those are like the core 4 rules. But how do you play? You must define penalties, fouls, and how to keep score. How do you know what's a foul without the core rules?

In the game of business, the CEO is like the referee.

The referee can't be in the middle with the players, playing the game, or they may squelch debate (*Rule 5, Vigorous Debate*) since they're not a peer. Guard against trying to be a player/coach as a CEO. If you're a player/coach how do you help others become their best (*Rule 6, Best Rule*)?

Do you have all the players you need? Recognize that the competency and gifts of some players in some areas is different. Recognize each value based on their role (*Rule 6, Best Rule*).

Know your role too. The Zig rule (*Rule 7, The Zig Rule*) is about how you assist others to score. There is a reason why in sports people who assist are recognized just as much as the people who score. Without the assist there wouldn't be a score.

Players want to play with and be coached by people who are committed (*Rule 8, Commitment Rule*). They want to know you have skin in the game, so to speak.

The end of every game should be celebrated, win or lose, because it's what keeps the team motivated (*Rule 9, Celebrate Rule*). You have to watch replays of your game so you can copy what worked, and learn from what didn't (*Rule 10, Learning Rule*).

Here is how rules 5-10 rest on one or more of the Core 4:

- Vigorous Debate Rule, rests on Trust and Safety
- Best rule, rests on the Golden Rule
- Zig Rule, rests on Profit First
- Commitment Rule rests on Trust and Safety
- Celebrate Rule rests on Safety and Profit First
- Learning Rule rests on Vigorous Debate and Trust

ACTIVITY 1 — THE RULES OF THE GAME

The Players

Who are the Players in your life? The relationships you identified in Module 3 are your players. List them here along with their classifications of 1-5.

What are the ground rules for these relationships? The ground rules are your core values, the ones that set the game, so these values will apply to all equally.

What are your rules/boundaries for your 1 and 2 relationships? These boundaries should reflect the value of these relationships. These rules and boundaries help you understand how to call a foul or a time-out.

Describe times when relationships with these players have gone outside the rules/boundaries, and what were the consequences? Have you defined the consequences of a foul?

Identify how your gameplay rules impact your 1 players.

Identify how your gameplay rules impact your 2 players.

Identify how your gameplay rules impact your 3 players.

Identify how your gameplay rules impact your 4 and 5 players.

What's The Point?

Defining boundaries helps us know what to say yes to and when, and what to say no to and when—as well as when we need to stop. Knowing this helps us live our why.

Takeaway

Continually acting against your own why by not knowing your boundaries, and not having clarity on your relationships, will wreak havoc with your life because you will be making commitments haphazardly. Ultimately, if you value your relationships, boundaries are there to protect them and help them grow and mature in healthy ways. They increase trust and help us recover trust when it's damaged and/or lost.

Resources

- *The 7 Habits of Highly Effective People*, Stephen R. Covey
- *The Speed of Trust* by Stephen M. R. Covey
- *Profit First* by Mike Michalowicz

CHAPTER 5

What Do You Value?

You have internal convictions that tie back to your **why**—what are those convictions? One of the things I value is time. Time is a commodity that you can never get back, and how you spend your time determines whether or not you live your why.

I also value relationships; in fact, relationships are central to my own personal why. That's also the basis for several of my rules, like the Trust Rule and the Celebrate Rule. See how everything ties together? My values influenced my why, then my why helped me clarify my values, which helped me create my rules.

Your values determine the guidelines by which you live. By determining our values, we can create a set of tools to help make decisions and practice our personal principles.

ACTIVITY 1   **IDENTIFY VALUES**

My Values

List your values, then order them by importance. Next to each value, note why it is important to you personally.

VALUE	WHY IT IS IMPORTANT TO ME PERSONALLY

Transforming Values into Core Principles

Determining what you value was just the first step. Next you need to develop them into core principles.

For example, like I mentioned before, I value relationships. Not just my own, but the relationships the people in my life have with their families and close friends. As a leader in the oil and gas business, one important principle associated with valuing my employees' relationships was keeping them safe at work so they could come back home to their families every night.

My core principle of Safety is a direct result of my value: Relationships. Values are statements, principles are how you live the statements.

ACTIVITY 2   IDENTIFY CORE PRINCIPLES

What core principles align with your values from activity 1?
List your values, then enter core principles that align with them.

CORE VALUES	CORE PRINCIPLES
Ex. Honesty	Ex. To always tell the truth, even when it hurts

How Core Principles Get You to Your Why— Your Destination

Now that you've completed this activity, think back to the Why statement you created in chapter 2. Do they go together? Does each principle support you living your why every day? If one of your principles is in conflict with your why, you may have conflict within yourself. Do you say one thing but do another? Do your audio and video match, or are you in an English-dubbed anime?

At this point it's not about how "good" your principles are, it's about how defined they are and if you are able to live them. If one of your principles involves staying at work late to get a project done, no matter what, but your why includes spending evenings connecting with your family, you have a conflict.

Your principles are your vehicle to your why. If your vehicle isn't meant for off-road travel, but your why includes exploring the wilds of Alaska, your vehicle isn't going to help you live your why.

ACTIVITY 3
CHECKING ALIGNMENT: TEST YOUR PRINCIPLES AGAINST YOUR WHY

Remember, your Principles are your vehicle to living your WHY. If your car can't accommodate your journey, it's not the right car for you. Write down your why, then list your principles from the last activity and evaluate how they do or don't align with your why statement.

Write your WHY from Chapter 2 here:

List your principles from the last activity. Do they align with your why?

PRINCIPLES	IN WHAT WAY DOES IT ALIGN WITH YOUR WHY?

Practicing Core Principles

How will you practice your core principles? These principles don't mean much unless you put them into practice. Living your principles and putting them into practice reduces how much or how often you are a hypocrite. I can hear you thinking, "What? I'm not a hypocrite!" You know that isn't true. We're human, which means that we will be hypocritical at times. Our goal is to reduce that as much as possible.

Once you've defined and tested your core principles, make a plan for how you will practice them on a daily basis. This might involve setting goals for yourself, like making an effort to be more direct in your communication with others or committing to treating others with respect and kindness.

Be mindful of your thoughts, words, and actions. Pay attention to how you interact with others and make sure that you are aligning your behavior with your values.

Look for where you failed to put your principles into action, and what you would do differently in those situations. For example, if honesty is one of your core principles, you might make an effort to be more transparent in your communication with your family or colleagues. Eliminating the word "try" from your vocabulary is one way to be more transparent in communication.

Take time to reflect on how you are doing in terms of practicing your core principles. This can help you identify areas where you are doing well and areas you need to work on. Life goes by so fast, if you don't take the time to reflect and learn, you forget what is important.

ACTIVITY 4 — IDENTIFY YOUR RULES

Turning your core principles into rules

Now that you've identified your core principles, and ensured that they align with your personal why, list each principle here. Make each principle succinct and actionable to create a rule. If the rule isn't actionable, no one can follow it. A rule also creates a boundary that helps you say "yes" or "no" to something that requires a decision.

PRINCIPLE	RULE
Ex. To always tell the truth, even when it hurts	Ex. The Commitment Rule. To "try" is not a true commitment. Either say yes or no, even when it hurts

What's The Point?
Your values determine your principles, becoming the guidelines by which you live.

Takeaway
Your principles are your vehicle to your why. If your vehicle is out of alignment, it's pulling you in one direction or another, not allowing you to easily go where you want. Having your values and principles aligned helps us get to where we want to go faster, and with fewer accidents.

Resources
- *Daring Greatly*, Brené Brown

CHAPTER 6

Vigorous Debate

In *The Seven Habits of Highly Effective People*, the practice of seeking to understand, then to be understood (which we will talk about in The Zig Rule) best describes the overall goal of the Vigorous Debate Rule.

The components of healthy, vigorous debate are: Defining the Question, Active Listening, Reflecting, and Trusting. Overlooking even one of these will hinder the process.

Defining the Question

Form a question around the specific thing to be debated. The person that brings the question, item, or thing to the debate, should present it in the form of a question. For example: How do we... How do I... Then the other participants will ask clarifying questions.

One of the key rules of clarifying questions is: don't suggest a solution. It's in our nature to want to solve problems, and it comes from a very good place, but listening and clarifying what the person is actually asking to get a full understanding of the situation is vital to this process.

As the umpire, a CEO's duty is to help everybody understand the rules of the game and let a team member know when they've gone out-of-bounds i.e., attacking a person's character rather than challenging their viewpoint. When questioning is done well, the individual expressing their feelings or beliefs will feel heard, even if others disagree. Remember, everyone's voices need to be heard—their viewpoint is vital in getting the best answer, or answers.

Active Listening

This takes training and discipline, and should be practiced every day. Human beings are emotional creatures and maintaining objectivity when someone is discussing you, your team, or something you're invested in is extremely hard. The key is to listen for the complete narrative without allowing oneself to become defensive and angry.

Reflecting

When the issue at hand has been clarified for all parties involved and the reasons behind each party's stance have been openly explored, the next steps are usually clear. When there are two divergent paths forward, and both have their merits, the CEO has to make the decision on which path is best for the team or company. I have found most of the time, if the umpiring has been done effectively, having to make a judgment is rare. When these steps are followed, the members of the team feel heard and respected. The team will move forward with clarity.

Trusting

If people understand the rationale behind what's been decided, they can still support the initiative even if they would have made a different choice. Everyone may not be happy or agree with a judgment call, but everyone will feel as if they have been heard and understood, and that builds trust. When a team has trust, there are very few limitations on the success the team can attain.

Examples of Vigorous Debate Rule

Brené Brown defines vulnerability as exposure, uncertainty, and emotional risk. The Vigorous Debate rule can be extremely difficult to practice, especially for a CEO who is a "know it all," like I was, complete with a roster of Sacred Cows (personal friends) who could not be challenged.

True vigorous debate requires that the CEO become vulnerable, exposing their ideas, leadership style, personnel, and organization to the uncertainty of what a team member might think. We naturally want to defend ourselves, our team, and our company when criticism occurs, even when that criticism is valid. To instead lean into the criticism and have an open and honest discussion about it, takes intention and discipline.

The CEO should not be a participant in the Vigorous Debate process. Rather, their role should be limited to serving as the umpire, so to speak. Training the team in the skill of seeking to understand before seeking to be understood. As a facilitator, the CEO brings topics to the debate process, as well as curates topics from issues brought up by the team.

Failing to implement

One day, Jim, my VP of Sales, had an honest discussion with me about how our 10 rules were failing. "I'll be honest with you Lloyd," he hesitated, and I could tell that the next words were hard for him, "they became a point of frustration for the team because it was clear they didn't apply to everyone equally. Rather than being an example for employees, the rules showed the hypocrisy of the, um, Senior Leadership."

I knew what "Senior Leadership" meant. He was talking about me.

After thinking for a moment, I realized he was right. There were several examples where I and others in leadership had acted hypocritically. But that's what the vigorous debate rule is there to prevent, isn't it? When I asked him as much, he replied that they did speak up and tried to initiate a Vigorous Debate, several times, but were shot down so many times that they gave up. That's an example of how leadership can squelch and suppress debate. If we don't listen, they quit talking.

ACTIVITY 4 — VIGOROUS DEBATE

The Rules of the Game

Remember how we talked about setting the rules for the game of business? The arena of Vigorous Debate is one of the most important places where you're going to implement these ground rules. The only things that should be debated are those things that are within your company's boundaries. For example, what if someone wants to debate if the company should increase the number of hours a driver can travel in one day before they're required to sleep because your company is having trouble meeting deadlines? If safety is one of your rules, that would not even be up for debate.

Then there are things within boundaries. What are the rules for debating those things? Following boundaries during a debate means that you debate with kindness, you listen, you ask clarifying questions, and you never offer a direct solution. The point is to talk it out. You should also stick to the topic at hand. To help with that, create a "Parking Lot" for items of discussion that may pop up during a debate that don't fit within the bounds of that particular debate. You can pull out that Parking Lot list at some point, and address those concerns in their own debate. That way, no one has to worry that their talking point will be forgotten.

The Rules of the Game for the CEO

There are some things that you, as the CEO, should never do in a debate. You should never bring a debate to the table if you've already made up your mind about the situation and you're just looking for confirmation. If you do that, you're going in with the desire to be "right." If the debate topic is one that you already have a strong opinion on, and are invested in a certain outcome, that's a situation where you should assign the "moderator" role to someone else. It's vital that the moderator be fair and objective.

If the team wants to have a debate, and it involves one of your Sacred Cows, or a situation in which you have a very biased viewpoint, and you cannot find a stand-in, it's your responsibility to work through that resistance to looking into the issue before you conduct the debate, otherwise you will squelch the debate itself and discourage team members from bringing up things that need to be addressed.

Your Turn!

Brainstorm a list of possible debates that might be addressed that fall within the boundaries of your values. Brainstorm a list of possible debates that might be addressed that fall outside your boundaries. In that second list, also include things that may come up in a legitimate debate that are outside of your boundaries.

DEBATES OR OUTSIDE MY BOUNDARIES	DEBATES INSIDE MY BOUNDARIES
Ex: Should we remove an item from the safety checklist to save time?	Ex: Do we need to hire a director of HR?

Turn it Around

Choose one of your debates that would be out of bounds and evaluate what could be changed to make it fit inside your boundaries. Look at your list of "out of bounds" topics and create a list of ways you could steer your team's Vigorous Debate in the right direction should someone bring up one of these topics. Brainstorm how you will address out-of-bounds questions and topics before they come up.

Debate!

Pick a debate from your "inside my boundaries" list and create a list of rules that should be followed for this discussion. Choose trusted advisors, or members of your cohort, and engage in the debate. Debate as the CEO/moderator, and then as a participant. Get comfortable with the differences. Practice being neutral.

Define What is Debatable

That's the role of the CEO, to determine the boundaries of the court, to facilitate the debate.

Established debate boundaries should be discussed before each and every debate. This is something that will be unique to each company's culture, and should be developed with the help of the team.

Time Frame

What is the time allowed for debate? Once everyone has been heard, and if there is a consensus, whose responsibility is it to follow through with the decision? And what is the time frame for it to be executed?

There is a time frame for each part of the process. How long to define the question? How long will you allow clarifying questions? Determine if this is an urgent issue, and the appropriate deadline associated with that determination.

What's The Point?

Communication is key to healthy relationships and a healthy organization.

Takeaway

Clarity is derived from making sure everyone is heard. The only way to accomplish this is to make sure your team members feel safe sharing their thoughts with you, and know that they're heard and their opinion is valued. Employees who don't feel safe don't share their valuable input.

Resources

- Brené Brown: *How to Rumble*.[1]
- *Fierce Conversations*, Susan Scott
- *The Advantage*, Patrick Lencioni
- *Trust and Inspire*, Stephen MR Covey

---

[1] This is a link to an online article. If you're reading a physical copy of this book, simply go to Google and search "Brené Brown How to Rumble" and it should be one of the first hits

CHAPTER 7

Best Rule

"The Best" is based on your own personal mark, or goal. As every individual is unique, so "The Best" is individual and unique. A CEO's job is recognizing the attributes, skills, and talents required to do a job, and then providing a minimum expectation to fulfill that role. However, the expectation is that the Mark for an employee will change over time as they perform the job.

Mark—A defined ability that is calculated by multiplying your God-given talents, and the investment in you by family, friends, educators, mentors, and self. Your Mark is unique to you and therefore the Mark is different for every person. The Mark should be ever-changing until the day you die. When we understand that each of us is totally unique, comparing ourselves to others is destructive. The best for one person is an individual measurement and can only be truly measured by our creator.

The CEO's job is to set the expectations for how the company's Mark is going to be implemented for it to be its Best.

The old adage, 'you can't manage what you don't measure' applies to the Mark.

Competency Scale

Determining an individual's or a company's best involves evaluating competency. Nature's law of repetition states that repetition creates competency. Noel Birch introduced a learning model in the 1970s as an employee of Gordon Training International called the 4 States of Competence.

The four states are: Unconscious Incompetence, Conscious Incompetence, Conscious Competence, and Unconscious Competence.

Unconscious Incompetence	Conscious Incompetence	Conscious Competence	Unconscious Competence
You are unaware of the skill and you lack proficiency	You are unaware of the skill but are not yet proficient	You are able to use the skill but only with effort	Performing the skill becomes automatic

Unconscious Incompetence is when you aren't competent in a skill, but you aren't even aware that it's a skill you should have. At this stage, you need to recognize that you don't know what you don't know, and strive to begin learning.

Conscious Incompetence comes when you know about a skill, and it's something you need in your life, but you aren't yet good at it.

Conscious Competence is when you've learned to do something, but you're still at that point where it requires conscious thought to complete the task correctly.

Finally, Unconscious Competence is something you can do well without thinking. For example, have you ever been driving home and thinking about something, then you realize you're home! You drove without even thinking about all the complex maneuvers required when operating a vehicle.

Measuring a person's or organization's "best" requires that you understand where they fall on the competency scale in whatever task you're evaluating. If you know that a person is consciously competent in a skill, you wouldn't compare their performance to someone who is unconsciously competent. It's not a fair comparison.

In a later chapter, we'll talk about the EDGE Method and how to use it to bring people from conscious incompetence to conscious competence.

Examples of The Best Rule

Striving for our individual and collective Bests keeps the team and organization healthy. The Best is not a standard, but an aspirational milestone unique to every individual and every company. It is ever-changing, based on where we are in our life cycle. Our physical, mental, and life experiences are always changing every day from the moment we are born until we die.

Internal Promotion not Based on Competency

I have a friend, Shawn Twing, who is a Labor and Employment Law attorney. He also represented our company on several occasions. Recently we had a conversation about promoting from within. He does training and consulting for companies as part of his legal practice.

He told me that in his training he asks the attendees, "Please raise your hand if you were promoted from within into your management position." The overwhelming majority raise their hand.

He then asks them to keep it raised if they received any management training prior to taking the job, and over 90 percent lower their hand.

As Laurence J. Peter defined in his Peter Principle: employees are promoted based on their success in previous jobs until they reach a level at which they are no longer competent, as skills in one job do not necessarily translate to another.

Another way of saying this is, **we take someone who is unconsciously competent in their current job and promote them into one where they are consciously incompetent, and sometimes unconsciously incompetent.** That is what Command and Control companies do with their team members, versus Trust and Inspire leaders.

What is a Command and Control company? It is a company where leadership says, "Congratulations! You've been promoted! Now, go and do your new job because we trust you based on your performance in your previous role." The person then fails because they haven't been trained in the new role using the EDGE method.

How can you expect someone to do better than their own personal best? Especially when it is your responsibility to identify and work with that "best"?

To promote from within, a company's training program must make sure that the employee is, at a minimum, performing their job by being consciously competent with the ability to become unconsciously competent.

Identifying this and creating training methods for internal promotions is a good way to practice the Best Rule.

Without using the EDGE method I mentioned above, promoting in this way is a command and control tactic, utilizing the "tell, trust" method, which leads to failure. We will dive more deeply into that in Chapter 14.

| ACTIVITY 1 | THE BEST |

Defining the Best

Now that we've learned how to define someone's best, let's look at some specific examples. First make a list of your own skills. Rate them as: Unconsciously Competent, Consciously Competent, and Consciously Incompetent. That will help you really internalize what those definitions mean. As an extra challenge, try to identify some things in your life where you may be Unconsciously Incompetent. You may have to ask your spouse or children for help on that one.

THINGS I DO IN MY DAILY LIFE	MY COMPETENCY IN THAT ACTIVITY
Ex: Making coffee	Unconsciously Competent
Ex: Programming the universal remote control	Consciously Incompetent

The Mark

Now I want you to consider your team members. If you're the CEO of a very large company, you might want to just pick a group of team members that you're most familiar with. For each team member, list one skill they have from each category.

EX: THINGS SARAH DOES ON THE JOB	HER COMPETENCY IN THAT ACTIVITY
Making presentations	Unconsciously Competent
Interviewing candidates	Consciously Competent
Photoshop	Consciously Incompetent
De-escalating situations	Unconsciously Incompetent

TEAM MEMBER	COMPETENCY

TEAM MEMBER	COMPETENCY

TEAM MEMBER	COMPETENCY

TEAM MEMBER	COMPETENCY

Let's get real

Considering your list, think of a situation where each of those employees didn't meet your expectations with any one of these skills.

Looking at the example I gave at the top of your list, how would you handle a situation where Sarah created something for the company in Photoshop and it was not up to your company's standards. How competent is she? From the list we made, it looks like she's Consciously Incompetent. Understanding this, was your expectation appropriate?

Did you consider her competency in Photoshop, or **did you simply need something, and asked her because she's such a rockstar in the boardroom?** We often see competency in one area, and assume competency in all areas, and that isn't fair to anyone. It's your job to evaluate competency, AND it's your job to teach them the things they need to know to do their jobs. Implementing the EDGE Method will help you do this.

Now, complete this activity for each of the team members that you included in your list and any of their skills that have been an issue in the past. Evaluate if your expectations were appropriate. Brainstorm how you could handle that situation better in the future. List whether this skill could be improved with attitude or aptitude. Consider what kind of training you could provide to increase competency.

TEAM MEMBER/SKILL	ATTITUDE OR APTITUDE	ISSUE/RESOLUTION
Sarah Photoshop	Aptitude	Sarah created a graphic in Photoshop and it was not good. My client was disappointed and it made both me and the company look bad. Looking at my list, I realize that even though she's great at presentations, she isn't competent in Photoshop. In fact, she probably agreed to do it just to make me happy. Is this something I want her to do in the future, and is this something she wants to do in the future? If so, I should look for Photoshop training and pay for her to take the class. If not, I should find another person to complete that task.
John Missed client's preferred deadline	Attitude	John doesn't create a deadline, no matter what the assignment is, and doesn't take responsibility for the outcome. He is always blaming others for their failures. In talking to him about it, it's clear he doesn't see a problem. If he can't be self-aware enough to understand why he failed, he should no longer be on the team.

TEAM MEMBER/SKILL	ATTITUDE OR APTITUDE	ISSUE/RESOLUTION

Attitude or Aptitude

On the subject of attitude versus aptitude, making this distinction is very important. If it's simply a matter of learning something, and they have the aptitude, then you can provide training. If they don't have the aptitude, then you may need to evaluate if they're in the right position, or if you can just transfer that one responsibility to someone else. If the question becomes: will their attitude allow them to become competent in this skill, and the answer is no, you may have a bigger problem, because attitude is a much more difficult aspect to manage. You cannot control another person's behavior and if their attitude is not good, it's going to impact the entire team.

What's The Point?

A person's best is based on their gifts, skills, and talents, and how it relates to their competency in that role.

Takeaway

A person's best is not measured against a generic benchmark, or even against other people—it is measured by their own unique gifts, skills, and talents. How well you train them determines how far their Best can take them.

Resources

- The 4 Stages of Competence, Gordon Training International. Original idea attributed to Noel Burch.[1]

---

[1] Adams, L. (n.d.). Learning a new skill is easier said than done. Gordon Training International. Retrieved April 20, 2023, from https://www.gordontraining.com/free-workplace-articles/learning-a-new-skill-is-easier-said-than-done/

CHAPTER 8

The Zig Rule

Zig's rule is the "what," and Stephen R. Covey taught me the "how."

While working with BJ Unichem, they sent us to a week-long corporate training using his book, the *Seven Habits of Highly Successful People*, as the foundation for the culture of BJ Services. "Seek to understand, then to be understood," is the foundation of learning what your customer wants. In order to seek to understand, you have to get really good at asking questions and become an active listener, which is the "how."

Alex was a member of my team who injured his back while on the job. He had a ruptured disc, and the surgery they recommended would mean this young man would have a 25-pound lifting limit for the rest of his life. He would have had to either change jobs in our organization, or find a new line of work entirely.

There was an experimental option to repair the disc using a spinal tap and a laser. But like most experimental procedures it wasn't easily approved. I ended up talking with HR to advocate for the approval and thankfully, they said yes, and the procedure was successful. Alex eventually left the company and continued working in the oil and gas industry.

When we ran into each other years later, I learned Alex had a successful amateur bodybuilding career, that he was an avid mountain bike rider, and had been living a very dynamic life. He'd also developed great management skills since leaving BJ Unichem.

Coincidentally, we had a need for someone with his skills, and he agreed to come to work for Smart Chemical in a field management role. He rose quickly into senior management and was an amazing team leader.

My goal at the time of Alex's surgery had been simply to help an employee get the treatment that would be best for his long-term success. I had no idea that, 20 years later, that same employee would become an outstanding leader in my own company.

My actions years ago helped Alex tremendously, and circled back around to help me and my company. That's the Zig Rule in action.

ACTIVITY 1 **THE ZIG RULE**

Helping Others

This goes back to your Why statement. If your purpose is serving others, and you don't help others get what they want, you're being hypocritical. You should be able to reflect on how you've helped others. Leaders who want to be served don't get this rule. Make a list of people who have helped you get what you want, and what was the impact on your life?

NAME	WHAT I LEARNED	HOW THEY HELPED ME, AND WHAT WAS THE IMPACT OF THAT HELP?

Make a list of a few people in your life who you KNOW you could help get what they want. You know what they want, and you either know how to help them get it or know someone who does. Write out what they want and exactly how you can help them get it. Extra credit: Choose one person every month and execute your plan.

NAME	WHAT THEY WANT	HOW I CAN HELP THEM

The next activity will be a bit harder. Think of a person who needs your help, who you have the ability to help, but you really don't want to. Explore why this is the case, because there is something there that you need to learn.

NAME	WHAT THEY WANT	WHY AM I SO RESISTANT TO HELPING THIS PERSON?

Lastly, when was the last time you did something unexpected for someone else that didn't benefit you at all, but benefited them? Do you have a lot of those instances, or just a few? Write out a description of when you've done that and how that felt. If there are many, or just a few—why? Journal those reasons, realizing that—while it may seem like the lack of a decision—choosing not to help someone is a decision.

What's The Point?
It's never about what you receive, but about how you serve others.

Takeaway
Helping others, when done with sincerity and integrity, will always come back to bless you.

Resources
- *Goals: How to Get the Most out of Your Life*, Zig Ziglar. For a video snippet of this, go to https://www.youtube.com/watch?v=kB7sDw5pMll 1:40
- *The Go Giver*, Bob Burg and John David Mann
- *The Traveler's Gift*, Andy Andrews

CHAPTER 9

The Commitment Rule

Definition, *Commitment*: the state of being dedicated to a cause or activity; a pledge."

Of all the rules, I believe that the Commitment Rule is really key to building a culture of success.

I think about the many times in my organization, and in my personal life, that I made or received a commitment and believed that we had an agreement. Unfortunately, I rarely took the time or effort to define what we were committing to. I didn't define the time frame or the consequences of success—or failure.

A commitment must be defined and understood by both individuals. Which means that you, as the CEO, need to define clear expectations before asking for a commitment or giving a commitment. Defining expectations for success and also for corrective action if we miss the mark is an integral part of every commitment, big or small.

The word "try" has no place in the world of clear expectation, that word is about as unclear as it gets. ***Try is a lie.*** And the truth is, **the person you're really lying to is yourself.** If you say you'll try, you're giving yourself permission not to do it. True commitment comes from conviction. If you're not committed or convicted, you will use the word try. If you don't think you will be able to get something done in the time frame proposed, communicate that to the other person, don't just say "I'll try" in order to avoid the pain of disappointment. **We don't want to let people down and in avoiding that, we just let them down even more in the future.**

Sometimes you have to admit that you aren't going to be able to do something because you aren't knowledgeable enough, you aren't gifted enough, or you aren't competent. When you are transparent and vulnerable with the other person, the opportunity to find the best way becomes an option, versus "trying." This might even include meeting those needs in a different way, possibly by bringing in someone to help you, or providing training.

In fact, you could—and should—ask yourself if there is a subject matter expert who is better suited to do this. There's a great book by Dan Sullivan that I talked about in the introduction to this guide called, *Who Not How: The Formula to Achieve Bigger Goals Through Accelerating Teamwork*, that addresses this very subject. Dan explains that sometimes, you don't need to know HOW to do something, you need to know WHO already can. Is there a professional on Fiverr or Upwork who could help you in areas where you're not competent?

In the end, good or bad relationships are defined and measured by whether or not we made, defined, and kept our commitments. I believe that all CEOs should be evaluated by this measure. When you make a commitment, you're saying that you will put forth your best effort and that you will follow through on your commitment. You plan for success, create contingencies for failure, and establish timelines for everyone involved to review the plan and how they'll keep their commitment.

The Three Commitments

These are the three most common types of commitments you will need to define and prioritize: Process Commitments, Vision Commitments, and Heart Commitments.

PROCESS COMMITMENTS

A process commitment involves agreeing to complete a task. A simple checkmark. It's either done, or not. This is the most common—and most broken—type of commitment.

The words "try" and "maybe" have become something people commonly use so they can have an "out" when being asked to make a decision or a commitment. When you're the CEO, people want to say yes to you. When they can't say yes, but are not comfortable saying no, they default to "I'll give it my best shot," or "I'll try," in order to try to placate you in the moment and figure out a solution later. Defining the commitment is the beginning of the commitment rule. It means that the organization, and you as its leader, have invested the time to think about and develop a process that is clear and repeatable.

Process-oriented commitments usually take very little time for clarification, yes or no should be the standard for this type of commitment. Examples are: picking up a package, changing the oil on a vehicle, calling someone, and other things we commit to routinely.

VISION COMMITMENTS

Vision commitments have longer time frames, more personnel, and more financial resources, and should therefore take more time to understand and define. "Due by" dates or evaluation dates for Vision Commitments are mandatory. Examples are budgets, construction projects, employee development plans, and maintenance contracts.

HEART COMMITMENTS

Heart commitment is the hardest, and the most important. This commitment level requires a leader to "dare greatly." In Brené Brown's book, *Daring Greatly*, she talks about being vulnerable and understanding that you're all-in and fully engaged when you take that courageous step into a Heart Level commitment. The heart decision is really a lifelong decision and doesn't have an end date.

> ***Examples of The Commitment Rule***
>
> *Remember my customer, Danny? He's a great example of how to do the Commitment Rule correctly.*
>
> *When he came to me and said, "I feel like such a hard ass sometimes." I asked him why he would say that he was being a hard ass when all he was doing was keeping people accountable for commitments that they'd made—commitments that were in writing. In fact, it seemed to me like he was being a good leader by having clear expectations and holding his people accountable to the commitments they made.*
>
> *This perspective helped him, because he hadn't thought of it that way. He was a kind man and worried that his hardline stance on commitments with the service companies he worked with was too harsh.*
>
> *In today's society, it seems to be so unusual for people and companies to keep their actual commitments, that when somebody holds others accountable to their commitments, they are a "hard ass" or mean. When in reality, holding someone to their commitments is one of the kindest things you can do.*
>
> *Danny saw himself as being blunt or callous. I and others, however, perceived him as being honest and direct. We always knew that he would do what he said, and that he'd make sure we did what we said. Something he saw as a weakness was one of the things I respected most about him.*

There is no try, only do

When my daughter Bailey was young, and had recently learned to drive, I tried to impart to her the importance of getting her oil changed regularly in order to keep her car in good condition. One morning at breakfast I asked her if she'd had her oil changed like I'd asked, and she said she hadn't. When I made it clear she needed to do it that day and no later she said, "Ok dad, I'll try." I explained to her how "try is a lie" and that if she wasn't going to do it, she should just say that rather than trying to placate me with the word "try." In the wise words of Yoda, "There is no try, only do."

ACTIVITY 1 — YOUR COMMITMENTS

Evaluating your Commitments

Think of all the commitments you have in your life. Make three columns: Process, Vision, and Heart to represent the three commitments. Classify your commitments based on the definitions you were given in this module.

PROCESS	VISION	HEART
Checking equipment at the end of my shift	Developing a long-term budget for my company or a major project	Speaking the truth, no matter what

Write down some memorable commitments. Evaluate if you set clear expectations, and what happened. If it was a negative outcome, what expectations would have changed that? If it was positive, how can you apply that process to other commitments? Evaluate failures involving commitments you've made in areas where you're consciously incompetent, and make sure none of your current commitments fall into that category.

Separate by kinds of commitment. You'll likely find a common denominator for the successes as well as the failures.

COMMITMENT AND TYPE OF COMMITMENT	WAS THERE A CLEAR EXPECTATION? Y/N	NEGATIVE OR POSITIVE OUTCOME	EVALUATE
Changing my oil Process Commitment	Y	Positive	I made an appointment for myself in my calendar every 6 months to make an oil change appointment and followed through.
Developing my "WHY" statement Heart Commitment			

THE COMMITMENT RULE | 103

What's The Point?
Keeping commitments is the ultimate builder of trust. Realizing that 'no' is just as much of a commitment as 'yes.'

Takeaway
If you commit with the phrase, "I'll try"—you aren't really committing. Committing with "I'll try" is a lie. You're only committing to a possibility. That's not a commitment at all!

Resources
- *The Traveler's Gift*, Andy Andrews
- *The Last Arrow*, Erwin Raphael McManus
- *The Speed of Trust*, Stephen MR Covey

CHAPTER 10

The Celebrate Rule

A shared experience around corporate celebration fosters real interpersonal connection. Think about the important events in our lives that we share with others: birthdays, graduations, marriages, funerals, holidays. If you're going to have a celebration rule, you have to be intentional by setting specific dates each year to stop and celebrate.

This is about enjoying the journey rather than just looking toward the destination. I mentioned a study in Chapter 4 that shows how groups who practice regular celebration (positive rituals) create stronger bonds. One study not only "...demonstrated that rituals lead to social bonding, but also provided support for the hypothesis that emotional state—and more specifically positive affect—is related to feelings of social connectedness..." [Charles SJ, van Mulukom V, Brown JE, Watts F, Dunbar RIM, Farias M (2021) United on Sunday: The effects of secular rituals on social bonding and affect. PLoS ONE 16(1): e0242546. https://doi.org/10.1371/journal.pone.0242546]

Celebrating builds relationships and creates memories that last a lifetime.

It's important to celebrate growth or change in your business. Then reflect on it and apply The Learning Rule. What failures can we learn from? What successes can we repeat?

That's how you integrate the Learning Rule with the Celebrate Rule. As a bonus, there's usually cake!

Examples of The Celebrate Rule

Earlier when talking about the Safety Rule, I explained how I decided that every month during my tenure as CEO, I would get a stack of cards for the employees who were celebrating a birthday that month. I took the time to handwrite each one, letting them know how special they were to me both as an individual, and as part of our team. When they received those cards, they felt valued because they knew they were worth the time that I took to write them. While that decision was made to honor the Safety Rule, it's also about the Celebrate Rule.

One day after my friend Jay passed away, I received a phone call from Christian, a mid-level team member. He was calling to offer his condolences. Christian knew how much my friendship with Jay meant, because of the connection we made through the handwritten cards and having met him at new employee orientation. There were so many times when I was the recipient of gratitude for writing these birthday cards, and like most times when you do something for others, I ended up getting blessed so much more!

The most important thing about celebrating an event like a birthday is that it really connects people. To celebrate, first you must take the time to recognize the individual and get to know them. In doing so, you inevitably become invested in that person and their future.

When creating a culture where you care about each other, you never know how that will impact you personally.

When we were developing our 10 Rules, the Celebrate Rule was included because we wanted to make sure that we acknowledged the contribution and value of our people, and that we memorialized shared experiences. The same is true when it comes to a business.

ACTIVITY 1   **LET'S CELEBRATE!**

Celebrating is about others

Celebrating isn't about you, it's about the other people. When we celebrate, we're practicing the Zig rule. What are things we need to celebrate in order to serve others by celebrating them? Celebrating people makes them feel seen and appreciated.

Let's go through a list of activities to help you understand how to celebrate in a more meaningful way…

What do you celebrate and why?

What do you celebrate with your family? With your team members? With your customers and clients? Why do you celebrate those things?

How do you celebrate?

Write out, in detail, how you celebrate those things. As in all things, having a clear understanding of how things actually are is the only way to make them better. Be honest. How much do you put into celebrations?

How could these celebrations be better?
Brainstorm how you could make these even more meaningful.

What else could you be celebrating?
Now, brainstorm a list of things that could be celebrated but aren't currently. Then describe how you would like to celebrate them. Then do it!

What opportunity to celebrate have you missed out on?
What is something that you missed the opportunity to celebrate and regret, and why. Is this something that happens consistently?

What's The Point?

Celebrating is about OTHERS, not you, and it fosters real connection. Not only that, but when you take the time to celebrate, you are focusing on today. You're enjoying the journey rather than just anticipating the destination.

Takeaway

"Nobody cares how much you know, until they know how much you care." — Teddy Roosevelt.

Celebrate the most important things in your life, and be intentional so at the end of your life, you have very few regrets.

Resources

- *How Will You Measure Your Life*, Clayton M Christensen, with James Allworth and Karen Dillon
- How To Celebrate Success At Work[1]
- How Celebrating Success Can Lead To More Of It[2]
- How Celebrations Affect Employee Satisfaction[3]

---

1 https://www.leapsome.com/blog/how-to-celebrate-success-at-work
2 https://www.forbes.com/sites/forbesagencycouncil/2022/05/12/how-celebrating-success-can-lead-to-more-of-it/?sh=1e26112b2eca
3 https://www.staples.com/content-hub/culture/holiday/how-celebrations-affect-employee-satisfaction

CHAPTER 11

The Learning Rule

When I wrote *Refined by Failure*, I started with Rule 10 to underscore the importance of recognizing the compounding effects that occur when you don't take the learning rule seriously.

When I was at pivotal transition points in my life and in my career, I always thought that THIS failure was going to be the one that ended my journey. As a CEO you rely on your intellect, experience, and logic to get you through those moments of fear, and this was no different. Not seeing this failure or that failure as a learning opportunity was my mistake. Identifying with your failures doesn't accomplish anything, learning from those failures moves you forward in life.

Viewing your failures as a part of yourself only brings shame, and shame is a very powerful state of mind. Brené Brown does an amazing job of helping define what shame is and what it's not, and learning about shame and the power of it helps you understand how it affects your decisions. This allows you to make more rational decisions, understanding that these transition points are opportunities to learn and get better rather than events that define who you are.

It is essential to learn that today is what you need to focus on. There is a quote by Eleanor Roosevelt, "Yesterday is history. Tomorrow is a mystery. Today is a gift. That's why we call it 'The Present.'" If the past freezes you where you are, it affects your future. If you are still living in the past, you haven't learned from it. If you didn't learn from the past, it prevents future successes. The very definition of insanity is doing the same thing again and again, expecting different results. Focusing on today is your biggest lesson. Learn from your failure then put it behind you.

Examples of The Learning Rule

Andy Andrews, one of my favorite authors, says in his book *The Traveler's Gift*, "God did not give you the discernment to make right decisions all the time. He did, however, grant you the ability to make wrong decisions right."

I have used the quote to validate and justify making quick decisions all by myself. I still believe wholeheartedly in this quote, because CEOs and leaders have to make decisions, and understanding this quote keeps us from analysis paralysis. However, if not careful, it can become an excuse for siloed thinking and rash decisions—the way it did for me. Making a decision based on our wants rather than focusing on what is best.

You can look at a propensity toward making rash decisions as a temperature check. If you're making a lot of rash decisions, it says something is wrong with your decision-making process. Rash decisions are made quickly, and without considering the consequences or how you're going to follow through with those decisions. When you make decisions with a sense of urgency, you're not taking the time to consider the consequences, and the outcome can be painful.

The silver lining is that the pain helps you learn.

This also ties back to the commitment rule. Sometimes rash decisions are a result of not understanding what level of commitment you're making. Heart commitments need much more thought than process commitments, for example. Every decision has a cost, and with rash decisions, that cost is often the pain of regret. Decisions based on conviction can be painful as well, but it's a good pain based on self-evaluation and reflection, not regret.

In applying the learning rule to the failures in my book, I've learned that many of the challenges I shared could've been minimized if I had followed these rules:
- Recognize that there is no shame in accepting counsel from those you trust.
- Create clear and defined expectations.
- Most importantly, hold yourself and your team to those expectations.

Application of The Learning Rule

Before you complete this next activity, I want to give you an example of something that happened in my life—a decision I made that didn't align with my values.

Three days after my daughter was born, I went to a corporate event in San Francisco. It wasn't a mandatory event, but I was busy chasing corporate success. I didn't think about it like this at the time, but I made this decision because I was focused completely on myself.

My wife's grandmother was in hospice at the time, and she very much wanted to see her great grandchild before she passed. After Bailey was born, we took her to see Lora's grandmother and for those three days, it was as if she was completely healed and whole. The light returned to her eyes and she was truly happy.

Immediately after that, I left for my trip. She passed away while I was gone. My decision to leave town caused me to miss the greater celebration of a new life, and the opportunity to share in the mourning of someone who had transitioned into the next.

If you were to ask me why, I would have to say that at the time, I valued my career more than my true treasure: my family. The advice I would give to my younger self would be: define and value your treasure.

ACTIVITY 1 — LEARNING THROUGH FAILURE

What would the person that you are today, tell the person you were 10 years ago if you had the opportunity?

Failing Up

This will likely have some repeats from an activity we did earlier, but that's ok. You're in a different place now—you know more now.

First, make a list of your most memorable successes on the following page. For each one, list:
- What did you do right?
- How have you applied that to future decisions?
- How can you apply what you learned to things you're currently doing?

Now make a list of your most memorable failures. For each one, list:
- What did you do right? (because it isn't always ALL bad)
- What did you do wrong?
- What lesson did you take away from that failure?
- How did you apply that lesson to future situations?

Finally, looking at your list of failures, define:
- What was the cost of the failure? List the cost in dollars, relationships, or influence.
- What was the hidden blessing?
- What value did you get from learning from this failure?

CHAPTER 12

The Importance of Boundaries

Why is all of this important? Why have rules at all? Let's dive into that. I've listed my core 4 rules below, along with questions about why they're important. I encourage you to examine your own rules in this way.

Profit First Rule
- What does this rule accomplish? This rule allows us to have fun. In fact, it was originally called the Fun Rule. When you make profits a priority, you're making people your priority, as counterintuitive as that may sound at first.
- What benefit have I seen from implementing this rule? When profits are safeguarded, your team members receive good pay, and good benefits, your investors see good returns, and you have a booming business.
- What have I seen happen when this rule was ignored? When this rule is ignored, you can experience losses that make layoffs necessary. Downsizing hurts each and every employee because those who are laid off are losing their source of income, and those who stay have to do more work.

The Golden Rule
- What does this rule accomplish? This rule ensures that we think of others first. This rule is others-focused rather than self-focused, which is the foundation for treating each other with respect. Treating someone with respect can be an ambiguous concept because we all may have different definitions of respect. However we can all understand how we would like to be treated.
- What benefit have I seen from implementing this rule? I've seen people disagree with one another without it turning into a personal attack. I have seen people do extremely kind things for one another over and over, and this kind of interaction builds trust.
- What are the consequences when this rule is abused? When this rule is abused, everyone becomes self-focused. This degrades trust, which is our highest value.

The Safety Rule
- What does this rule accomplish? This rule has one purpose: to make sure you go home to your loved ones every night after work. If you don't go home, nothing else matters. This rule focuses on the intrinsic value of human life, and the consequences that would occur if a team member or coworker is injured, or dies.
- What benefit have I seen from implementing this rule? This rule helps team members realize that they are responsible for one another, and have to take an active role in everyone's safety, not just their own.
- What have I seen happen when this rule is ignored? When people are hurt, families are changed forever, and the company suffers financial and sometimes civil and criminal penalties.

The Trust Rule
- What does this rule accomplish? This rule recognizes the most valuable asset a person or a company has: trust. That's why this is the basis for all the other rules. When you have trust, following the other rules has purpose, which is to give and earn trust.
- What benefit have I seen from implementing this rule? I've seen team members build trusting relationships that allowed negotiations and debates to go smoothly and actually accomplish their goal, because everyone trusted one another enough to know that everyone had their best interests in mind.
- What have I seen happen when this rule was ignored? When this rule is ignored, everyone becomes a lone wolf, only looking out for their own personal interests. The consequence of that is that any rules you have become nothing more than "token" rules, because no one believes in them. When your rules become empty and meaningless, they give you a false sense of security. If you can't trust that other people will follow the rules, that impacts every other rule. They have little to no value. How can you trust someone's best if they're only focused on themselves? How will they commit, serve, or debate? It's the cornerstone of any rule or value you implement in your company because without trust, rules mean nothing. Lack of trust destroys the foundation of a company.

Failing Inside Boundaries
Failing inside boundaries is when you tried to accomplish something within the bounds of your WHY and your RULES, and it didn't work out. This may have been due to unclear expectations, or simply not considering your competency in that matter, causing you to fail. This is an opportunity to remind yourself that failure is an event, not a person. You then simply apply the learning rule. Evaluate what went right, evaluate what went wrong, and create a stronger approach that you can use in the future. Failing within your boundaries is safe, because the consequences of failure have already been identified and

the tools needed to apply the learning rule are in place. We're not jeopardizing the company or the people in a catastrophic way.

Failure within boundaries is generally a failure that you can recover from. Failure within boundaries usually doesn't undermine trust. Trust is a difficult thing to recover, once lost. Failing within your boundaries is not catastrophic.

Failing Outside Boundaries

Failing outside your boundaries leads you to one question: "Why?" Why did you make the decision to do something that violated your core values that you want to protect? If you have taken the time to establish values, boundaries, and rules, failure in this arena is not a matter of "unconscious incompetence." This is a conscious decision to violate your own values and to break trust.

That doesn't negate your value, nor does it change the fact that failure is an event, not a person. If you allow the shame of past failures to influence the situation, **you won't apply the learning rule, and then the failure is compounded.**

An example of failing outside boundaries would be a situation in which you felt you had to lie to someone to get what you wanted, despite honesty being one of your values. Someone cheating on their spouse would be violating the Trust Rule, the Commitment Rule, and many others. The consequences of failing outside boundaries are much more severe because these failures involve breaking trust, which may not ever be regained.

Jordan Peterson has a video series that explains how trust is your most valuable currency. He illustrates this by considering a situation with a married couple. They may have been married for years and years, and in those years, they've built up quite a lot of trust. However, you can negate 50,000 hours of trust with just 30 minutes of unfaithfulness. That seems extreme, but think about it. One action can destroy decades of trust and faithfulness.

Evaluating and Learning from Failure

We're conditioned by society to view failures as personal attributes. Shame over what happened clouds our vision and prevents us from learning. That is the true failure. But it doesn't have to be that way. Like I've reminded you during this course, Failure is an Event, Not a Person! Evaluating and learning from your failure means that it wasn't in vain. Learning from your mistakes is the most valuable gift you can give yourself.

Objectivity is key. Think of a really emotional failure, one that has been clouded by shame. The failure that you can't think about without feeling that pit in the middle of your stomach. We need to be analytical in evaluation versus focusing on the emotion tied to our failure.

First, separate that failure from who you are as a person. If it helps, create an imaginary person and pretend they did it. This is just to give you some distance, and also help you see how you might feel if someone else committed the offense or made that decision (we're often much more compassionate with others than we are with ourselves).

Next, evaluate what went right, and what went wrong. There's a saying: "Even a broken clock is right twice a day." There are almost definitely decisions you made in that situation that were right. Think about those and remember to keep doing that! Now think about the decisions you made that were wrong. How were they wrong? Was this failure inside or outside boundaries? What kinds of situations could you possibly face in the future where you could make the same wrong decision? What decisions would have resulted in success? How can you implement those in the future?

This is how you turn failure into learning. This is how you make sure that you get all of the benefit and learning from the cost of your failure. This is how you fail less, and succeed more.

| ACTIVITY 1 | DEFINING BOUNDARIES |

Identifying Obstacles to Working Within the Rules

Identifying any obstacles you may have to working within your rules is vital to their success in your company, and in your life. You might wonder why you have to identify obstacles if you are the one who wrote the rules! However, we all have values and ideals that may be hard to live up to from time to time. Just because you know you should treat others the way you would like to be treated doesn't mean you aren't occasionally tempted to talk about someone behind their back.

List your rules. Next to each rule, think of any obstacles you might face when trying to honor that rule. Identifying these is vital, because you can't address what you can't see. After you've identified your obstacles, write out ways you can overcome them.

YOUR RULES	YOUR OBSTACLES
Vigorous Debate	It's hard for me to step back and allow my team to debate issues with other team members who I have a close personal relationship with.

THE IMPORTANCE OF BOUNDARIES | 119

Overcoming those Obstacles

What's The Point?
Clearly defining your boundaries is the beginning of being a trustworthy person. It helps you know when to say yes, and when to say no.

Takeaway
Your boundaries are how you intentionally steer your life and without them, how can you have a life of purpose?

Resources
- *The Purpose-Driven Life*, Rick Warren
- *The On-Purpose Person*, Kevin W McCarthy
- *Who Not How*, Dan Sullivan and Dr. Benjamin Hardy
- *Never Split the Difference*, by Chris Voss. Here's a quote from the book:
- "Research shows that the best way to deal with negativity is to observe it, without reaction and without judgment. Then consciously label each negative feeling and replace it with positive, compassionate, and solution-based thoughts."
- That's how we address our obstacles: without reaction or judgment. We then brainstorm how to overcome those obstacles with positive, compassionate, and solution-based thoughts.

CHAPTER 13

Communicating Rules and Values

How do you set the anchor that is establishing new rules and values? How do you communicate that to a group of people?

Story.

People learn through stories, in fact, that's how we've learned for millennia. Stories help make ideas personal and actionable, which makes it easier for people to remember and implement.

StoryBrand is a marketing technique developed by Donald Miller. He took the basic "Hero's Journey" framework, created by Joseph Campbell, and applied it to business. Now, this is generally applied to the customer journey. But how would that work if applied to the real heroes of the story: your individual team members?

The StoryBrand framework follows this plan:

- A Hero
- Has a problem (there are internal problems, like philosophical obstacles, and external, like other people or events outside your control)
- And meets a guide
- Who gives them a plan
- And calls them to action
- Which leads to success
- And avoids failure
- And achieves transformation

Pretty good, right? We're just going to make one tweak, and I'm sure you can guess which one we'll change. "And **avoids** failure" in a workplace story should be "And helps them **learn from** failure."

How to Apply This Technique

- The Hero: this is each employee or team member. You can think of this as a personal StoryBrand for each and every person, where **they are the hero** of their journey in your company. Their quest is to execute their responsibilities while abiding by the set boundaries to the best of their ability. It's very important to remember that the CEO is never the hero. **You are the guide**, the facilitator. What would happen to an organization where the CEO was the hero, if that CEO stepped down, or died? The entire organization would be vulnerable.
- Has a problem: the internal "problem" would be fellow employees, and external would be customers. But in our scenario, the "problem" is really the question: "how do I treat these people on my journey? What are our boundaries with one another?"
- And meets a guide: this is you, the CEO, the creator of the rules by which this company abides.
- Who gives them a plan: The overarching plan is your company Why Statement. The supporting plan includes your values.
- And calls them to action: This is The Rules list. If you've put a lot of thought into your rules, they will be an actionable roadmap for implementing the company Why and Values. How do these values and rules make their quest better?
- Which leads to success: This would include things like working with people you trust, who trust you. Knowing that your coworkers will do everything in their power to make sure you come home safe at night. Bonding with your coworkers over shared celebration, and on and on.
- And helps learn from failure: The Learning Rule. This is a workplace where failures are transformed into lessons that can be used to improve.
- And achieves transformation: This is transformation into a workplace with firmly defined boundaries and values, trust, celebration, lots of profit, helping others, true commitment, true understanding of capabilities, safety, having others treat you the way they want to be treated, the ability to respectfully debate, and learning from failure instead of being defined by it.

So how would that look if implemented with some of my rules?

John from accounting (**hero**) has to collaborate with Maggie from HR on a project for a client. The **problem** is that they don't agree on how they should move forward (internal issue, since they are coworkers, external, the client project).

Because the CEO (**guide**) has given them **a plan** (Why Statement) that prioritizes helping others and being a person of influence, they know that they will have to work together to make sure that whatever route they take, it truly helps the client and establishes them as an influential presence in the client's life. They can't focus on looking good to the boss, or getting their own way, because those run counter to the Why Statement.

They have internalized The Rules (which **call them to action**) due to the fact that they were woven into every interaction and every part of their daily experience in the company since they were hired.

Because of that, they immediately know that they will need to implement Vigorous Debate to solve this issue.

Because of their familiarity with the other rules, like the Trust Rule, and the Golden Rule, they can debate within the respectful boundaries that are in place and come to a compromise (**success**). If any **failures** occurred in the process, or if any occur during implementation, they implement the Learning Rule to ensure that the failure was as valuable as possible.

They've **transformed** their client's business success as well as their company's relationship with the client as a result of their project!

Take the above example, based on my rules, and make one according to your own rules and values.

Everything you've done so far has prepared you to implement your own rules based on these examples. You, as the CEO, have to live and breathe the rules.

Personal Accountability

To have accountability you have to be vulnerable. Vulnerability is very hard for someone in a C-Suite position because it can be used against you so easily, but you cannot be held accountable if you aren't vulnerable. This is why having trusted advisors, a mental coach, and employees you trust is essential. Be a trust and inspire leader, not a command-and-control CEO.

Personal accountability refers to your commitment to live the rules so others can follow your example. If you aren't practicing accountability, your company won't follow the rules/values. You have to give team members the permission and expectation that they'll hold you accountable when you do make decisions that don't live up to this. The goal is to never become the emperor who has no clothes.

Personal accountability starts with your yes meaning yes, and your no meaning no. It starts with commitment and trust—so much so that you invite constructive criticism from your trusted advisors and trusted team members. Give trust earn trust works both ways. It's as much for you as it is for them. It's a moral truth. This will attract those of like mind and repel those that aren't committed.

Aligning Behaviors to Values

Behavior is a result of the way you handle positive and negative stress. We have to retrain our behavior when we make a commitment to values, and sometimes things don't "fit" the same way as we retrain our brain, and thus, our behavior.

Have you ever pulled an old pair of shoes from the back of your closet and put them on? I have. I found an old pair of shoes that had been my favorites—I'd worn them every day and thought they looked and felt great. My excitement quickly turned to disappointment when I put them on. They just didn't fit right anymore. My feet had adapted to other shoes and their shape wasn't the same as before. Not only that, as I looked at my reflection in the mirror, I saw that they didn't look as nice as they did before, back when they were in style. Now they just looked old and outdated, and didn't feel right on my feet.

That's what happens to your old way of living when you begin to align your behaviors to your values, and truly start living your values rather than just giving them lip service. Things you used to do, people you used to hang around, places you used to go won't feel the same. They won't fit anymore. They won't look as attractive as they used to. And that is okay! That means you're growing!

Coaching Through Failure

This is coaching to fail, because failure is learning. Failing creates knowledge of what you don't know and what you need to become better at. A company whose goal is not to fail will **never grow**. Our incorrect assumption is that failure is bad. ***The only failure that's truly bad is a decision that was made outside the safe boundaries we've set,*** because that puts what we value at risk.

The number one thing in this process is trust. A failure that erodes trust is a true failure, versus a failure that helps us learn what we don't want to do. That failure doesn't erode trust—we just recognize that what we did didn't work and we need to develop more competency or do something different.

The only failure that may be unrecoverable is one that results from intentionally breaking the trust rule. All other failures can be navigated.

When a team member fails, it's generally not an intentional breaking of the trust rule. It is usually a failure to implement something correctly. When you promote a line worker to a manager because they're great at being a line worker, you're moving someone from a place of unconscious competence to conscious incompetence. You're setting them up for failure unless you recognize what their True Best is, and work from there. What do they know? What do they have the capacity to learn? How can you implement the EDGE Method to make sure that they are consciously competent in the things you assign to them? Don't wait for a project to fail before evaluating their competency.

Plan to Declare and Share: How will you communicate your story to your team members, customers, and organization?

PART ONE

First, go to www.mystorybrand.com and write out a brandscript, but remember that your team member is the hero, coworkers and/or customers are the "ideal client" and you, the CEO, are the guide. Use this to help you write your story for your team.

PART TWO

Declare your rules and share them with the team. You'll want to start by writing out exactly what your rules are, and write them in the way you want to present them to your team. You could just give them the list, but using a story like we talked about in the beginning is going to make more of an impact.

Once you've written out exactly what you want to say, take the time to internalize it, memorize it. Practice saying it out loud, from memory, in front of a mirror, or with a trusted advisor. Once you know it backward and forward, meet with your team. They'll see the ease with which you talk about these rules and values, and see that you've fully internalized them. In fact, after memorizing and practicing, it's likely some of this will begin to show up in your conversations and interactions with others. This is authenticity. The values you communicate verbally are the same values you communicate in every other way.

What's The Point?
Story is how we connect. It is the oldest form of communication, even before the written word.

Takeaway
You communicate values every day, whether by word or by action. Writing your story internalizes it, gives you ownership of it, and lets you see that it is possible. You can't achieve your dreams unless you dream.

Resources
- The StoryBrand website[1]
- **Building a StoryBrand**, Donald Miller
- The free worksheet[2] to build your own StoryBrand
- *Thirst*, Scott Harrison

---

1 www.storybrand.com
2 https://mystorybrand.com

CHAPTER 14

The Tell, Trust, Fail, Shame Box

How do you lead? Are you a dictator, or a guide? Most organizations are what Stephen MR Covey defines as "command and control" organizations. They tell their people to do something without teaching or guiding them, then trust them to figure it out, which almost always leads to failure and shame. If this is your leadership style, I'm not implying that you're setting your team members up for failure intentionally. Many leaders think they're trusting people by operating this way, but this method is actually disabling.

This process can turn into a vicious cycle really quickly. You tell an employee to do something with no more than a brief explanation, then you trust they can figure it out with little to no guidance. Sometimes we even provide a checklist, thinking that is enough instruction, but if they don't understand the desired result of following the checklist, it actually becomes a source of distrust, not trust. When you trust someone who has no competency (i.e., guidance/education), they're going to fail, and that failure leads to shame. That shame is multiplied when they're disciplined for the failure, despite the fact that they may have had no competency in that area, and no learning occurs. Moving forward, they are afraid to fail again, so they don't reach for anything new or ask to learn anything new. It's too risky.

Do You Lead a Command and Control Organization?

When I work with my coaching clients, some of my favorite tools are the whiteboard and PowerPoint presentations. I feel I can explain things so much better when I incorporate visuals. Below is an example of a PowerPoint presentation I use to lead my clients through an exercise aimed at discovering what kind of leader they are. Look over the following slides, and I'll dive into the information afterward.

IS YOUR ORGANIZATION

COMMAND AND CONTROL

OR

TRUST AND INSPIRE?

COMMAND AND CONTROL

- Managers make all decisions (top-down)
- Information is shared on an as-needed basis
- Checklist
  » Provided as the way to do things
  » Provided to create accountability
- Training is an event instead of a daily process
- One-way communication is the norm, whether it is in-person or written. Telling what is wanted or expected rather than showing or demonstrating

COMMAND AND CONTROL

- Compliance
- Transactional
- Efficiency
- Status Quo and Incrementalism
- Fixed Mindset
- Coordination among Functional Silos
- Control, Contain
- Motivation
- Manage People and Things[1]
- Use checklist
  » Ask if they understand
  » Tell people we trust them based on who they are not on their competency and training
- Failure is handled with:
  » Discipline
  » Shame
  » Yelling
  » Aggression
- Motivation comes from: a fear of failure—not from understanding both the reward of the success and the cost of failure

[1] This list is from Stephen MR Covey's *Trust and Inspire*

TRUST AND INSPIRE

PRINCIPLES
- Commitment
- Transformational
- Effectiveness
- Change and Innovation
- Growth Mindset
- Collaboration among Flexible, Interconnected Teams
- Release, Unleash
- Inspiration
- Manage Things, Lead People[1]

COMMUNICATION
- Communication: Uses the EDGE Process
  - » **E: Explain and Educate**
    Define success, as well as the cost of failure
  - » **D: Demonstrates How to Do**
    Use checklist as a map for success
  - » **G: Guides while team member does**
    Use checklist to train for competency
    Use checklist to learn what went wrong when a failure happens
  - » **E: Enables after a base competency has been established**
- Inspiration serendipitously happens because trust is the foundation

[1] This list is from Stephen MR Covey's *Trust and Inspire*

The Presentation

Let me dive a little deeper into the information on the slides.

When you assign responsibility to a team member, you give them a checklist and a goal and let them take it from there. They tell you, "I can understand the checklist, sure." Then we tell them we trust them—because we hired them and we figure they must be good people, right? But just because they're good people doesn't mean they're competent in a specific task. With nothing more than a checklist providing accountability, they feel abandoned and incompetent, which leads them to flounder and fail. The response to failure is yelling, pain, and aggression.

In a situation like this, your team member is negatively motivated to follow the checklist so they don't get in trouble, not so they can succeed and grow. They don't understand the underlying concepts of the task, just the steps to get there. In a command and control organization, people are given information on an as-needed basis. In a trust and inspire organization, everything is explained with the EDGE process.

We're educating them and not withholding the critical things that help them become successful. You have to ask yourself: do you trust the employee based on the control you know your company has over them? Or do you trust them because you know that you've helped them have the competency to understand it? You trust them to go do it because they're doing it for the success of the company and themselves, not for the fear of losing their job.

When they're educated with EDGE, the fear of losing their job is minimized because they have a greater understanding of the why and how in contrast to just a checklist and consequences. Permissive failure within boundaries creates a high-trust organization. Moreover, when team members do fail, because they have been provided the tools to understand why they failed and learn from it, they become more competent and failure doesn't repeat itself, leading to personal and corporate success.

In a command and control organization, team members are told that if they execute the checklist well the company will be successful—but they don't know why. It's about keeping people in the dark. With trust and inspire, team members know why the process exists, and understand the benefits of success as well as the cost of failure. Trust and inspire helps people see the full picture.

With the EDGE Method, team members learn what happens when failure occurs. Failure should happen during the learning process, then they can use the checklist to learn when and why they failed. That is why there is a guided learning portion to the process. They aren't given full responsibility for the task until they're 80 percent competent; they will become more competent through practice and learning from their mistakes. The goal is for them to exceed whoever trained them. In fact, giving the task to the team member when they've reached the point where they're 80 percent as competent as the person who trained them is the real way for a company to continue to accelerate and grow.

"Tell me and I forget, teach me and I may remember, involve me and I learn."
—Benjamin Franklin

The EDGE Method

The opposite of the Trust, Tell, Fail, Shame Box is the EDGE Method. I first heard about this method from a client of mine who was an Eagle Scout. We were talking about business and how to bring your people from conscious incompetence to conscious competence, and he began to tell me about the process they used. The EDGE method is what highly effective teams, from the Eagle Scouts to the elite Navy SEALs, use to create competency within their ranks. There is no telling and trusting going on. The SEALs must trust one another with their lives, and it takes serious training to create unconscious competence like that.

The EDGE Method

- **E** Explain/Educate
- **D** Demonstrate
- **G** Guide
- **E** Enable/Empower

The EDGE Method is a replication process creating real competency. EDGE recognizes that when learning something new, people are consciously incompetent. The E, explaining and educating, and D, demonstrating, move them from consciously incompetent to consciously competent. That is where

G, guiding, comes in, helping them move even further through that process. Then we E, enable them, knowing that while they're not 100% competent, they're at a place where when they fail, it will accelerate their learning and move them toward unconscious competence.

Checklists

Before we get further into The Edge Method, let's lay the groundwork for success, and talk about checklists.

A checklist ensures that everyone follows the same procedure every single time they complete a task. I was flying on a private plane with a pilot who had fourteen thousand hours of flight time. Think about that, FOURTEEN THOUSAND. This man had flown so much that it must have been second nature. Despite that, I noticed that he followed his detailed checklist before takeoff. He then had another detailed checklist that he followed when we got to altitude, and another for landing.

Sitting next to him, I couldn't stop myself from asking, "Why do you still use checklists when you've had so many hours of experience? Isn't this something you could do in your sleep?"

His answer wasn't what I expected. He said, "I don't trust myself."

"Why?" I was truly puzzled.

"Three words: normalization of deviation."

I still didn't understand.

He went on, "I don't trust myself, because in this line of work, the cost of failure is too great. When you don't follow your checklist, you risk the normalization of deviation. That phrase describes what happens when you deviate from your normal procedure—when you skip a box on your checklist. If you do it often enough, that deviation becomes your normal. I follow every single box in my checklist so that doesn't happen."

That was sobering. In his line of work, it is indeed too great a risk, lives are on the line. That's true for so many jobs, especially those that use any kind of equipment that can injure people, or worse. And even if the cost of failure doesn't mean lives lost, it can mean clients lost, relationships lost, trust lost, and financial consequences.

When considering the cost of failure, you can see that it's equally important to follow a detailed checklist when running your own company day to day. To follow the checklist even when it becomes mundane and routine. Say you're the CEO of a construction company. If your client hired you to build their new office and the construction crew staked it out without measuring, how much would it cost to go back and correct that once it was clear there was a problem? Wouldn't it be so much better to simply follow a detailed process, no matter how redundant it may seem?

After the pilot introduced me to the idea of "normalization of deviation" when he explained why he followed his checklist, I began to think about how often it occurs in my line of business. Say I had a detailed checklist for looking over our equipment at the end of the day to make sure everything was in good repair. I've been doing this for so long I can do it with my eyes closed. One day I'm in a hurry, so I skip a few steps in the checklist. Nothing bad happens. So the next day I skip those same steps again. Nothing bad happens. Pretty soon my eyes just skim right past those steps and I never do them, because skipping them has become my new normal.

The problem is, those steps are there for a reason, and at some point it will matter. As in this example, there could have been a major safety issue, not to mention the lost time and productivity when the equipment failure would have been preventable if the checklist had been followed.

Defining the Cost of Failure

There are three basic costs of failure: money, time, and reputation.

I want to talk about the greatest cost of failure: **reputation**. This isn't to bring shame into the conversation—we just need to talk about how failure impacts your reputation so that you can focus on ways to strengthen and maintain it. When failure occurs, it impacts your personal reputation, those of your team members, and that of your business.

Money and time are the fruits of having protected your reputation—which means that the focus must be there. In *Secrets of the Vine*, Bruce Wilkinson explains that the "fruit" is never the purpose—it's the result of the purpose. When God is in our life, and we're connected to Him, the fruit of that is a result of our connection to Him. Focusing on the connection is what produces the fruit.

Identify the Cost of Failure

- **Revenue** — What is the cost or loss in revenue from the failure and what is the cost to redo or make it right?
- **Time** — How much time did the process take initially, and then how much time was taken to make it right?
- **Reputation** — What is the impact of the failure to the following reputations?
    - » **Company** — What effect does the failure have on the company's reputation and how long does it last? **If it's posted on social media it can last forever.**
        - *How does this impact investors and/or financial partners?*
        - *How does this impact future business partners?*
    - » **Client** — What is the impact of the failure on our clients' reputation?
        - *How does it impact how they see themselves? Do they feel responsible for making the decision to work with your company?*
        - *How does it impact how others see them? Do others blame them or lose trust in their decision-making?*
    - » **Personal** — What is the impact on relationships for the owner or the employee, both inside the company and with those outside the company?
        - *External reputation of the owner or employee(s) involved in the failure? How long does it last?*

- *Internal reputation of the owner or employee(s) involved in the failure? How long does it last? How do their co-workers and/or executives perceive them?*
- *How does it impact how the owner or employee(s) feel about themselves? Does this failure create shame and fear?*

We need to really understand the full effect of this longest-lasting and greatest cost of failure. For most if not all humans, loss of reputation is one of our greatest fears and therefore needs to have processes to protect it. If there are established processes, even when there is failure, it doesn't impact your reputation or cause shame. Therefore, we feel safe about our reputation, our clients are protected, the company is protected, and our time is more efficient and more valuable. By protecting all of these things, the company will be compensated and achieve greater results. Protecting reputation is the foundation for a successful business, and ensures that it will be a Trust and Inspire Organization.

Protecting your business and employees' reputation ties back to the Core Four: valuing people. When you protect the reputation of the people you work with, you're protecting them from the consequences of failure. Using the EDGE Method to fully educate people on the "why" behind what we do, "how" to do it, and then teach them so they do it well, is the best way to protect reputation. An established process is the most efficient way to do that. You can focus on protecting your money, or protecting your time, but if you do that, you're missing the larger picture. Thoroughly educating and training people is about protecting their reputation, and yours.

Going back to my conversation with the pilot, did you know that almost all plane crashes tie back to someone deviating from the established process? Think about that, hundreds of lives lost in one crash because someone got used to skipping a few steps in their established process.

The EDGE Method

E: Explain and then Educate

Education is the first step in the EDGE method and consists of thoroughly educating your team member about the task at hand. Educate and explain. Make sure that they know the ins and outs of the entire procedure, not just their own part in it, so they understand how their role ties in to the whole. You can do this by starting with a process flow diagram. That visual aid helps them see and understand where the process takes them to the point of success, then you can bring in the checklist to educate them on how to actually implement the process.

D: Demonstrate

Next, demonstrate. When you learned how to drive, even before you started, you were drawing on a lifetime of demonstration. In your driver's ed class, you received even more demonstration as the instructor drove you around a bit, explaining what was going on. They also showed you videos of people driving, and in some cases allowed you to use a driving simulator to experience the process before actually doing it.

Explanations and manuals are wonderful tools, but nothing beats watching someone do something that you're trying to learn. Baking is another great example. Maybe you grew up watching your parents or grandparents cook. At some point they likely gave you direct demonstrations of what they were doing and why, while going through the recipe (checklist) with you.

G: Guide

After you demonstrate, it's time to let them try it with your guidance. This process involves the education and the demonstration, only this time they're in the driver's seat with you there to anticipate possible mistakes, correct any mistakes they may make, and keep them safe while they practice and build confidence.

E: Empower and Enable

This is a crucial step. Once your team member goes through the first three steps, if done correctly, they're becoming consciously competent, moving toward eventually becoming unconsciously competent. Now is when you give ownership of the process over to them. This not only gives their work meaning, but it continues to solidify the process in their minds. At this point, they assume the role of guide. When another team member needs to go through the EDGE method to learn this process, they will be ready to walk them through it, causing them to think even more deeply about the process until they become a true expert in that operation.

How to use EDGE within the story framework

Like we discussed before, using story is the most effective way to communicate with people. The EDGE method ties in with the "And give them a plan" portion of the hero's journey. As the CEO, it is your role to facilitate, to give them a plan and trust them to enact that plan. However, recognize that training is the foundation for execution, otherwise you're just setting everyone up for failure.

What's The Point?
Awareness of how you lead allows you to choose between being a Trust and Inspire leader or a Command and Control leader.

Takeaway
Training using the EDGE Method ensures competency and ultimately creates a foundation for each team member to achieve their Best.

Resources
- How to Teach Using the EDGE Method, RapidStart Leadership[1]
- How to use the EDGE Technique to Lead Your Team, RapidStart Leadership[2]
- To Teach with the EDGE Method, Academic Paper on acadamia.edu[3]

---

1 RapidStart Leadership. (2015, September 8). How to teach using the edge method - 2-minute tip. YouTube. Retrieved April 20, 2023, from https://www.youtube.com/watch?v=t16YcpmR3HU
2 RapidStart Leadership. (2016, March 22). How to use the edge technique to lead your team. YouTube. Retrieved April 20, 2023, from https://www.youtube.com/watch?v=6TflsOdILHI
3 https://www.academia.edu/39502891/To_Teach_the_Edge_Method_Use_the_Edge_Method_or_EDGE_and_TWI_

CHAPTER 15

Writing Your Story

At the beginning of this guide, there was an activity focused on having you write your own story. I mentioned that we'd be writing a different story at the end—a story of intention. Now that you know and understand yourself, your values, your principles and your true intentions, we're going to write a story about what will happen to your personal and professional life three years after implementing your rules.

Imagine this: It is three years in the future, and you've fully implemented your rules. What will your company look like? How will your employees feel about working there? How will the public see your company? What will your finances look like?

If you're familiar with Cameron Herold, author of *Vivid Vision: A Remarkable Tool For Aligning Your Business Around a Shared Vision of the Future*, this will sound familiar. Writing your Vivid Vision creates a clear and in-depth description of how your business will look and feel in three years, as if it's already happened.

In his book, *Vivid Vision* (which I highly recommend), Cameron shares:

"One helpful exercise is to imagine that you're filming every aspect of your business: your employees, customers, supplier relationships, and so on. Play the film in your mind: What do the big-picture details look like three years out?"

The key is to imagine how it feels and what it looks like, not how you'll get there. That's the sticking point for most entrepreneurs when writing a Vivid Vision document. They may say, "In three years, my revenue will triple." But then when they think about it, they get caught in the loop of: how can I increase revenue, what will I need to do, if I could increase my revenue that much, wouldn't I have done it already? It's impossible. At that point, you've just defeated yourself. Focus on what you want, not how you'll get it.

Activity: Vivid Vision

Challenge yourself to think outside your comfort zone! Write down what you would like to see in each part of your business, as if it's already happened. Do this for every part of your business, which I've listed below.

In *Vivid Vision*, Herald states: "Once I had put on paper all the ideas in my head, I was then able to write a three-page description of all the thoughts I had generated through mind-mapping. I organized them by such areas as marketing, finance, IT, operations, customer service, employee engagement, and so forth."

Create a description of what you want to see, as if it's already happened, for each of these areas:

- Core values
- Team
- Culture
- Products & Services
- Sales & Marketing
- Media & Awards
- Financials

Set aside a time with no interruptions so you can really dream. I know that's a tall order, but make an appointment with yourself and respect it as you would respect time with someone else. Grab a notebook and pen, or your laptop or tablet, whatever medium allows your mind and ideas to flow best.

Think about your company, and pretend it's three years from now. Imagine you're in the office on an average workday. What do you see? What do you hear? How do you feel? What is the atmosphere like? Be very specific while also keeping in mind you're just describing what you see, not the steps you took to get there.

Display It

Once you have written your Vivid Vision, it should be printed and circulated throughout your organization, and should be placed in a prominent area for all team members to see and read on a regular basis. Send it via email, frame it and put it in the breakroom. Present it to your staff during a meeting and tell it like a story, their story. Because they are the heroes in this visionary story.

| ACTIVITY 1 | VIVID VISION |

Writing your Vivid Vision

The following is the text from a free download on www.vividvision.com. For additional suggestions and information, we recommend downloading this template directly from Vivid Vision's website listed above.

[Your Company Name] **'s Vivid Vision**

[3 Years From Today]

Snapshot

The following is *[my/our] [insert year]* Vivid Vision.

Creating a Vivid Vision brings the future into the present, so we can have clarity on what we are building now. It's a detailed overview of what *[my/our]* business will look like, feel like, and act like three years out—by *[month] [day], [year]*.

Why I Do What I Do *[Or: Why We Do What We Do]*: *[short, only 1-3 sentences around your why/core purpose.]*

Core Values

What values do you see being practiced? *[4-5 total values, 1-2 words each. Include 1-2 sentence descriptions for each value.]*

Culture

What is the culture like? *[Paint the picture. Use sensory language. What does the team culture look like? What does it feel like? What does it sound like? Are there any incentives for growth? Opportunities for personal/professional development?]*

Team/Employees

[Who is the driving force behind the business? List specific key roles, if applicable. What is the main function of each of these individuals? What do employee reviews on Indeed, Glassdoor, etc. say about the company?]

Activities OR Products/Services

[Ex: What does your company do? Give each product/service its own section and describe what it looks and feels like. What is your USP (Unique Selling Proposition)? What are you doing to stand out from your main competitors?]

Operations

[What does your HR department look like? Customer Service? How do your customers describe you as a company? What do your online reviews say?]

Offices/Headquarters *[Do you have an office? Imagine walking into it... Where are you (town, city, or state)? What specifically do you see? What do you hear? How do you feel? What do you smell? What do you taste?]*

Sales & Marketing *[How do you attract your ideal clients? What does your marketing strategy look like (SEO, Social Media, PR, Word of Mouth, etc.)? Give specific examples, if possible. How has this been successful?]*

Media & Awards *[What is the media saying about your business? What specific awards have you received? What specific articles have been written about you ("Top 10 Places To Work, As Voted By Employees In [Region]," "Fastest Growing [Industry] Companies")? Have you been mentioned in any reputable online magazines? If so, which ones (Forbes, Inc. 5000, etc.)?]*

Financials *[What are your sales? Yearly revenue? Profit? What is your annual growth rate?]*

Community Involvement/Giving Forward

[What specific local or global charities/organizations do you support? What does this look like? How do you support them (monetary donations, physical participation, etc.)? Why do you support them?]

Founder Feeling

[Option 1: Who are your mentors? What does personal growth mean to you and what does this look like? How do you spend your time? What does your day-to-day look like? How do you feel?]

[Option 2: How did you get into this industry/business? Share your story, what motivated you to start your business and why the work you do is important.]

[Optional: Include your signature.]

Bonus Sections
*To include ONLY if relevant to your business

Advisors

[How do your coaches, lawyers, accountants, etc. describe you?]

Suppliers

[How do your suppliers describe you as a company to work with?]

Engineering/IT

[What does this department look and feel like?]

Conclusion

This entire guide has been focused on one question: are you being intentional about creating your story or are you just letting it happen to you?

The processes and activities you've gone through are all tools to help you write your story. Will you do this? Will you write it? Or will you let it write itself and be carried along, eventually looking back, regretfully, on a life lived with no intention?

Finally, ask yourself this: did I take my time? Did I really allow these concepts to fully develop in my heart and mind as I went through this guide? I truly hope the answer is yes. If you feel maybe you didn't, or that you did, but not as fully as you would like—read it again. Do the activities again. It will be eye-opening to compare your activities from the first time to the second time.

Remember this, life is a journey. You have a decision: Will you write your own story, or let life write it for you?

Acknowledgments

I would like to acknowledge the people who have helped me along my coaching journey. To my wife Lora: You are more than just my partner in life, you have also helped me become a great coach by giving me a safe place to practice before working with my clients. We've learned how to navigate boundaries in both a coach and client relationship, as well as our husband and wife relationship.

To my clients: Just know that I couldn't be where I am today without you. The amazing conversations and revelations that we've had in our sessions together have allowed me to learn more than I ever thought possible. In the wise words of Yogi Bhajan, "If you want to learn something, read about it. If you want to understand something, write about it. If you want to master something, teach it." This has proven itself time and again and I expect it will continue to prove true as I share the lessons that I've learned with clients and others, and then learn from their lessons as well.

I also want to recognize Dan Sullivan and Dr. Benjamin Hardy, authors of *Who not How*. This book wouldn't even exist if it weren't for their valuable advice to find your who when you don't know how. Because of that advice, I reached out to April Kelly, one of the editors who helped me with my first book, *Refined by Failure*. If she hadn't come aboard, I would still be mired in working on the how of expressing all of the amazing revelations I've had. April, thank you so much for saying yes.

Lastly, I can't write acknowledgements without mentioning Stephen MR Covey. He was instrumental in the writing of this book because he defined trust, the process of establishing trust, then how to maintain it—and when trust is lost, how to regain it. I literally wouldn't be sitting here right now if it hadn't been for his impact on my life. All I can say is that his influence has been immeasurable.

At the end of the day, I'm just a funnel, distributing the knowledge and wisdom I'm blessed enough to receive from all the amazing people in my life.

ABOUT THE AUTHOR

C. Lloyd Brown

CEO Coach, co-founded Smart Chemical Services, an Oil Field Chemical Services Company in 2008. In 2017, Smart Chemical won the Inc. 5000 award for one of the fastest growing companies in America and won the award again in 2018 and 2019. In 2020, Lloyd stepped down as CEO assuming the role Vice Chairman of the Board.

In 2021, Lloyd released his first book, *Refined by Failure*, *Breaking Rules* and *Getting Burned*. He founded the Coaching Practice, Refined by Failure. The coaching practice works with Entrepreneurs, Executive and Business Leaders and their teams.

Lloyd received a B.B.A. in Petroleum Land Manage-ment from Texas Tech University in 1987.

Other experience includes Risk Management with CBIZ specializing in Group Captive Insurance Programs.

He currently serves on the Amarillo Economic Development Corporation and is a former Chairman of the Board. In August 2022, Lloyd is a member of the Rawls Business School Advisory Council at Texas Tech University.

Lloyd is a Facilitator for the Founders Group at the WT Enterprise Center and also serves as a mentor for Elevate Amarillo.

Lloyd is married to Lora and they have a daughter Bailey.

www.ingramcontent.com/pod-product-compliance
Lightning Source LLC
LaVergne TN
LVHW070531070526
838199LV00075B/6755